METAPHYSICAL DICTIONARY

1997

Canadian Cataloguing in Publication Data
Tangas, Sunny, 1940-
Metaphysical dictionary

ISBN 0-9681770-0-X

1. Spiritualism--Dictionaries. 2.Occultism--Dictionaries. 3. New Age Movement--Dictionaries. I.Title
BF1407.T36 1997 133'.03 C97-910064-X

Published by:
K.T. Publishers
Unit 178, 230-1210 Summit Dr.
Kamloops B.C. V2C 6M1

Printed in Canada

DEDICATED

TO

EMMANUEL MARIA STACEY DARREN

CONTENTS

ACKNOWLEDGEMENTS

I have been working on this dictionary for the last ten years. Everyone who knew I was building this dictionary sent me new words they had used or heard. All of these words have been carefully researched and sorted to make this dictionary possible.

With approximately 5000 words in alphabetical order, this dictionary will help those on their spiritual quest.

In Metaphysics, there can be many meanings for one word. Throughout this Dictionary there are entries that state they have "many meanings." These meanings may be contradictory to one another because different cultures and beliefs do have different meanings for the same word. I have put all the different meanings that I received into the Dictionary to widen our understanding of these words.

May your God Bless You
Sunny Tangas

ABOUT THE AUTHOR

Sunny Tangas was born in the small town of Chip Lake, Alberta, Canada. She is one of ten children raised on a farm in the 1940's.

Some of her hobbies are woodcarving, writing, painting, music and walking for hours in nature. The animals of the wild will come to her, without fear, to be petted and fed.

Metaphysics have been a great part of her life. She has a strong belief on the Ancient spiritual ones who have guided her with this dictionary.

Sincerely
Gail Ross
Co-chairperson
K T Spiritual Society
Kamloops B.C.

A

AARON'S ROD—a rod believed to be endowed with Metaphysical powers, a term now used in Dowsing.

ABARIS—said to be the teacher of Pythagoras who is believed to have lived without eating or drinking. He claimed to have the arrow of Appolo which gave him the ability to travel through the air and become invisible. A great Metaphysician of his time. see Pythagoras.

ABERRATION—a ghost-like vision of a person or object. Unnatural appearance or behaviour of non-physical energies.

ABEYANCE—a temporary lapse in spiritual growth because of one trying to hard. Lack of spiritual growth or desire.

ABIOGENESIS—spontaneous origination of living organisms from lifeless matter through spiritual means.

ABLE-BODIED—having a strong physical, mental and spiritual body, necessary for spiritual advancement and growth.

ABLUTION—a ritual of washing negative energies away from the body. Both religious and spiritual.

ABOMINABLE SNOWMAN—alleged being living in Tibetan Mountains. A large creature, not human but walking upright. Also known as Yeti.

ABORIGINAL—the first of its kind in all lands. Believed to live hand in hand with the Deities.

ABRACADABRA—the name of the supreme God of the Asstrians of the third century. A magical word often appearing on amulets. A word used in many rituals and casting of spells.

ABRAHAM—the Patriarch of the Hebrews in the Christian Genesis.

ABRAHAM THE ASTROLOGER—a 12th century astrologer who wrote many books on astrology, translated into Latin by Pietro d'Abano.

ABRAXAS—supreme God of the Gnostics who had the head of a king and the feet of serpents. Word of power.

ABSENT TREATMENT or HEALING—healing or treatment completed by transferring energy to the one requiring the healing. The healed need not be present.

ABSOLUTE—the ultimate reality of the universe, God, Buddha or Christ. The source of all that appears to the senses. The supreme deity from which all proceeds and to which all returns.

ABSOLUTE THRESHOLD— the border between physical and spiritual senses. The smallest point where the physical senses detect spiritual sensory stimulus.

ABSTAIN—to refrain deliberately from certain functions, often with effort of self denial, such as remaining celibate to gain greater spiritual growth.

ABSTRACT—that which cannot be touched or seen with the physical senses . A quality thought apart from any particular object or thing. Unclear in the physical or psychical realities.

ABSTRACT REALITY—all realities in altered states of mind, such as meditation or dreaming.

ABYSS—canyon or chasm. The Christians believed this to be the home of their negative entities such as Satan. The Goddess believes this to be the dwelling place, recycling centre and resting place of their great Goddess.

ACARYA—a Sanskrit word for one who teaches by ones own example, a spiritual master.

ACCEPTANCE—a state of mind which allows others to live their lives as they choose. Living daily with that which one has. To endure without protest or reaction.

ACCLIMATIZING—familiarizing or adapting oneself to the feelings and sensations of new Metaphysical practices by doing many practice exercises.

ACCURSED—being under a spell or curse. One who has deliberately been the subject of directed supernatural powers for the purposes of wrong doing. See Voids.

ACHARYA—a spiritual teacher of specific Metaphysical topics.

ACHILLES HEEL—a vulnerable point of one's physical body. (taken from the Greek war hero, Achilles, who killed Hector then himself was killed by an arrow to the heel.)

ACIHUAT—the Aztec "water woman," the lady of the Eastern waters of the underworld. see Llorona.

ACTIVATING A DIVINING OBJECT—the process of energizing and cleansing a divining object such as a crystal, tarot cards etc. through meditation and visualization.

ACTIVE FINGERS—a belief of many Dowsers that only some of the fingers of each hand have dowsing abilities.

ACTIVE INTELLIGENCE—the intelligence in the universe which is available to all humankind. Spiritual creative energy. see passive intelligence.

ACTIVE PSI—the phenomenon of making things happen which have no scientific explanation such as dowsing, psychic healing etc. see Psi.

ACTORIUS—a stone found in the gizzard of a capon and

worn as an amulet representing courage. An avian pearl.

ACUPRESSURE—an Ancient healing technique in which finger pressure is applied to necessary sensitive points on the body.

ACUPUNCTURE—a technique in which small needles are inserted under the skin to activate the flow of "Chi". Particularly effective as an anaesthetic with very little pain. Originated in China. Also used in Egypt, the Northern Eskimos and the Brazilian Indian Tribes.

ACUPUNTURE POINTS—points or sites along the skin where energy channels come closest to the surface of the skin.

ACU-YOGA—a healing method that combines accupressure and hatha yoga.

ADAM—Christian belief that this man was the progenitor of the human race. The first man of humankind.

ADAMANTIUS—(300 A.D.) a Jewish Doctor who founded physiognomy. (reading facial features.) see physiognomy.

ADAMSKI, GEORGE—(1891-1965) believed to be the one who brought the subject of U.F.O.s to world wide attention and the first to have claimed to be taken aboard these spaceships.

ADDITOR—a ouija board modified with a small round hollow box and a pointer protruding from it, which serves as a cabinet that moves under the fingers over a smooth board printed with the alphabet.

ADEPT—one who has outstanding knowledge of spiritual laws and the instructions of the application of these laws. A highly evolved master.

ADJUSTABLE SENSITIVITY DETECTOR—a tool used in Dowsing.

A straight wand made of a spring, with a bobber on it's end, which can be telescoped in and out of its handle. see Dowsing.

ADI—the first. The atomic plane of the solar system. The highest of the seven spiritual planes.

ADRENAL GLAND—the location of the solar plexis chakra. The fight or flight gland. The location of the sensors for picking up magnetic ray emanations which cause a dowsing response. see solar plexis chakra.

ADVANCED SOULS—those spirits or spirit entities who come to earth with a life plan and are able to live and enact these plans without creating future karma. Spiritual beings who help others complete their chosen physical experiences on this plane of reality.

AETHER—the ancients believed that this substance pervades the entire universe, similar to the ether of modern psychics and physics.

AFFIRMATION—a desire to change or add to oneself through statements spoken in the present tense and repeated several times in a ritualistic manner. (in conscious or altered state of mind.)

AFOCHE—African Santeria ritualistic dances. Often performed for tourists in Rio De Janeiro.

AFREET—an oriental term for the spirit of the dead which are generally negative and to be avoided.

AFTER-DEATH ENVIRONMENTS—the reality, level or place one's soul, or spirit, enters after physical death. A place far more intense and more joyful than the previous existence where new laws apply which are far less limiting.

AFTER DEATH TRAINING—a level of existence

where the soul or spirit goes to prepare for the next existence. A spiritual plane or place of education.

AFTER-IMAGE—the temporary remaining visual shadows on one's inner eyelids when one closes their eyes after looking at something. This is the form of images which appear when psychic imagery is attempted.

AGAPE—a Greek word for self-giving love. A word now used for "divine love" in most metaphysical and spiritual beliefs.

AGAPE LOVE—universal love where the primary purpose is that of a helping nature. Love that requires nothing in return.

AGE—a designated time of change. An apx. span of two thousand years in Metaphysical terms. see age of Aquarius.

AGE OF AQUARIUS—an age of enlightenment, spiritual growth and great love. The time when the sun moves into Aquarius. see age.

AGENT—the one who sees an object and acts as the sender or transmitter during a telepathy test.

AGLA—an acronym (Aieth Gadol Leolam Adonai) used by Kabalists to invoke demons.

AGO—robes worn in Nigerian spiritual rituals.

AGOGO—a bell used to call in a saint or Orisha in African Ritual. see Orisha.

AGPAOA, TONY—(1939-1982)the one who began the still popular psychic surgery in the Philippines, some believed him to be a quack. see psychic surgery.

AGRICULTURAL RADIESTHESIA—the use of Dowsing to answer questions as to where to plant certain agricultural crops.

AIR—one of the four elements. Air symbolizes alertness, clarity of perception and intelligence. see elements

AIR SIGNS—the astrological air signs are Gemini, Libre and Aquarius.

AKA—a Huna word meaning the connecting link between all life. An astral, ectoplasmic substance which conducts vital life forces and thought form impressions. The Huna believe this is what makes all divination possible. see Huna.

AKASHA—the realm of the spirit. That which permeates all space. The ether. The fifth element. That which fills the space between objects in the universe. Same as AEther. see fifth element.

AKASHIC RECORDS—records kept in the realm of the spirit that have knowledge of all events past, present and future for all mankind. A complete memory of nature.

AKKADIAN-CHALDEAN INSCRIPTIONS—documents from the Royal Library of Nineveh of the seventh century B.C. The oldest known magical writings which are mainly exorcism against evil.

ALBERTUS MAGNUS—(1193-1280) regarded as the most learned man in the middle ages. Influenced by Aristotle. He was one of the first to write about the therapeutic values of plants. He also wrote about talismen, magic and the occult.

ALBUMSAR—(885A.D.) an Arab writer who wrote on Astrology and Divination.

ALCHEMY—the art of transformation. The study of transforming oneself from one level or state of mind to another. The ultimate goal in Medieval times was to create the "philosopher's stone"

which would turn base metal into gold. Also to create the Elixir of Life, curing illnesses and conferring youth on those who drank it.

ALCHINDUS—(873 A.D.) an Arab physician, astronomer, mathematician and philosopher who wrote such works as On The Rays Of the Stars, etc.

ALEXANDER HEALING TECHNIQUE—a physical body healing technique which involves balance. "The head leads and the spine follows," is the main feature of this healing technique. Physical re-education to improve posture, thus releasing distorted beliefs and emotions.

A-LEYS—(archeo-astronomical leys) psychic energy lines found between heavenly bodies and sacred stones.

ALGORITHM—another term for the laws of nature, the manifestation of the spiritual networking.

ALIEN PERSONALITIES—a term used, mainly by Dowsers, meaning a person which has been possessed by a foreign or unwanted spirit. see walk-in.

ALIENS—intelligent beings from other bodies of the universe that many Metaphysical people believe are among us. Their main purpose is to teach us the different levels of reality and spirituality.

ALIENATION—the act of leaving or walking away from something of great importance to one, as in the loss of spiritual contact.

ALIGNMENT—the establishment of a path of least resistance for the flow of energy. Relaxing in a meditative state and making the mind, spirit and body as one.

ALKORAN—short version of the Koran, the sacred book

of the Moslems.

ALL THAT IS—another term for one's God or one's Deity.

ALLEGORY—a symbolic story or drama in which the characters and the complete story represent emotions or ideas, other than their literal natural meaning. Treatment of an illness by inducing an opposite condition.

ALLOPATHIC—using alternative medicine for preventing or treating any or all illnesses.

ALPHA—an altered state of mind where a light form of meditation takes place or begins. A Greek word used to mean the beginning. The first letter in the Greek alphabet.

ALPHA WAVES—a state of drowsiness, relaxation and lack of attention brought on by these brain rhythms. Alpha brain waves have a frequency range of 8-12 Hz (cycles per second)

ALTERED STATE OF CONSCIOUSNESS (ASC)—a state in which the usual balance of consciousness and subconsciousness is changed, when the consciousness is subdued and the subconsciousness takes over. i.e. hypnosis, etc.

ALTRUISM—helping and loving others with no interest of payment or recognition. Helping others grow in spirit without the need of payment.

ALVEN—a fairy or helpful spirit originating from the Netherlands, who assists in growing beautiful night blooming gardens.

AMAZONS—a tribe of Warrior Women, which, in ancient mythology were believed to live along the Amazon River.

AMEN—a Hebrew word used in early Egyptian rituals meaning "so be it."

Amen-Ra was the name of the Egyptian sun God. A word often used in modern day churches.

AMBROSIA—many meanings. The elixir of life in Ancient Mythology. Red wine of the Fairies. A Hindu term for body. The re-creative power of the Goddess belief.

AMEN—a word meaning "verily"in modern religous groups. The origin of the word is found in the Sanskrit aum and om. Introduced into the Ancient Egyptian mystic rites to express the hidden and invisible Gods.

AMERICAN ASSOCIATION OF NATUROPATHIC PHYSICIANS—P.O.Box 2579, Kirkland Wash 98083. A holistic health movement founded in the 1980's.

AMERICAN SOCIETY FOR PSYCHICAL RESEARCH—an organization founded for the purpose of recording psychic data. Founded in 1884 in Boston.

AMPERE'S THEORY OF MAGNETIZATION—Metaphysical theory which assumes that magnetic properties are due to the molecules circulating in the molecules of a magnet.

AMETHYST—the stone of spirituality and contentment which transforms lower energies into higher clearer energies.

AMMA—a spiritual form of massage used in Japan.

AMPHIGORY—an impressive sounding nonsense statement which has great meaning to one who understands it. See speaking in tongues.

AMULET—a spiritually charged object believed to be a focal point of protective energy. Often worn by one for protection and guidance. see talisman.

ANACHITIS—a stone used in Ancient rituals which aroused water spirits.

ANALOGUE SCALE—a Dowsing tool, usually ones own body, i.e. one foot of body height could equal ten feet of depth. The outstretched hand is usually the marker.

ANALYTICAL MIND—the thinking, computing portion of the mind. Left hemisphere of the brain. The mathematical as opposed to the spiritual side of the brain.

ANAPHRODISIAC—a substance which lessons sexual arousal.

ANATTA—the oldest and first Buddhist doctrine asserting that individuals do not possess eternal souls. see anatman.

ANATMAN—the modern Buddhist doctrine of the existence of man and woman's spiritual and eternal soul. see anatta.

ANCESTOR WORSHIP—religious and spiritual beliefs associated with relatives who have passed on or died.

ANCHOR—the energy attached to, and left on, the one being healed to carry on the effect of a spiritual healing.

ANCIENT BELIEF—the beliefs of the Ancient People of China, Egypt and Japan where one lived on a daily basis with daily instruction of the Deity.

ANCIENT BRAIN—that part of the brain programmed with existence in the early reptilian ages. The early spiritual brain used for existence.

ANCIENTS—The spiritual masters, mentors and highly evolved teachers of Ancient time. It is said that we are guided by these Masters in these modern times. Spiritual persons from the early 1900's who guide us in the present. Spiritual ancestors.

ANDROGYNOUS—the belief that male and female energies occupy all living things. The Goddesses believe that many of their creative Goddesses were androgynous.

ANEBOS—an Egyptian prophet to whom Porphyry wrote the famous imaginary letter, questioning divination, incantations and other paranormal arts. A reply exists. see Iamblichus.

ANGEL—a Greek word meaning messenger. Heavenly beings who send messages between the Deity and humankind. An entity without a physical body which helps and assists in one's physical and spiritual journey.

ANGEL OF DEATH—a belief which originated from Judaism about the being who extracts the soul from the body at the moment of death.

ANGELOLOGY—an in depth study of angels in all beliefs, from all areas of the universe.

ANGLE—in Astrology this is the cusp of the first, fourth, seventh or tenth houses. This is either end of the horizon or the meridian.

ANGLE RODS—any Dowsing device, coat hangers or copper tubing, consisting of two L-shaped rods, one to be held in each hand. When the rods cross this indicates a Dowsing response.

ANIMA—the contrasexual complex in the male.

ANIMA MUNDI—ancient term meaning animal magnetism. The soul of the world idea as accepted by ancient mystics. see soul of the world

ANIMAL MAGNETISM—many meanings. The belief that the life process or existence of all kind has a soul or measurable substance. The theory upon which Christian Science was based. Spiritual forces.

ANIMAL REINCARNATION—the belief that animals reincarnate into different animal lives, as do humans, and that all animals must grow spiritually.

ANIMATE—all things or objects that are living and growing, such as plants, animals, minerals and humans. Having the ability to move about in the physical reality.

ANIMISM—the belief that all objects possess a natural vitality, that all objects possess living souls.

ANIMUS—the contrasexual complex in the female. see anima.

ANIMAL MAGNETISM—an early name for what is now called "hypnosis", based on the idea that therapeutic effects could result from altered magnetic fluids of the body.

ANIMISM—the Metaphysical belief that all life was, and is, produced by a spiritual force, that the physical and spiritual bodies of all life are separate yet one.

ANKH—ancient Egyptian cross, shaped as a Christian cross with a half circle at it's top. This symbol signified life, combining the masculine and the feminine. Dowsers believe the Ankh cross was used for Dowsing.

ANPSI—the ability of animals to experience paranormal events. (precognition, telekinesis, etc.)

ANTAHKARANA—the spiritual path or bridge between higher and lower minds. A mental bridge.

ANTHROPOMAGNETOMETER—a term Dr. Jaboj used to describe a dowser. His theory was that dowsing depends on the human sensitivity and reaction to minute changes in ones magnetic field of the aura.

ANTHROPIC PRINCIPLE—the belief that this universe was created by the Deity particularly suited for human life.

ANUBIS—an Egyptian jackal-headed God representing the evolution from lower to higher levels of consciousness.

APHRODISIAC—a substance such as essential oils, which produces sexual arousal.

APACHE TEARS—an obsidian stone traditionally representing the tears of Native woman mourning for their warriors driven from a cliff by the cavalry.

APOCALYPSE—a literary genre in which mysterious revelations were explained by a supernatural being such as an angel.

APOCRYPHA—books of the Christian Bible accepted by the Catholic Church and yet rejected by the Protestants. Fourteen books which form a bridge from the Old Testament to the New Testament, which the Puritans disagreed with and are no longer in print.

APOSTLE—a person with special knowledge, from the Christian belief system.

APOSTOLATE—a student of many different studies, generally associated with the studies of the deity.

APOTHEOSIS—the official act of classifying a human as a god because of some heroic or humane act.

APPARATION—the unexplainable appearance, feel or sound of a person, animal or thing which does not inhabit the usual three dimensions or conform to reality as it is understood. A ghost.

APPOINTED ASSEMBLY—a group or council of highly evolved spiritual beings who are chosen to represent individual planets.

APPORT—objects which materialize out of thin air, especially at seances. The ability to create or move objects without physical contact, distance has no bearing on this action. An object alleged to have arrived in a closed space, indicating the supposed passage of matter through matter. see teleportation. see asport.

APRIL MOON—known as Shower moon by many cultures because of the many warm April showers. see Shower Moon.

AQUA VITAE—a term used by alchemists meaning ether. see ether.

AQUAMARINE—a variety of "beryl" which crystallize prismatically. Called the stone of courage which enhances rapid intellectual response.

AQUARIAN AGE—when the position of the sun on the vernal equinox, moves through the path of the zodiac westward for apx. 2000 years, this period is referred to as an age. When it crosses into the sign Aquarius, the Aquarium age will have begun.

AQUARIUS—the Zodiac sign "the water carrier" January 20-February 18.

AQUASTATS—lines of anomalies or mineral veins of underground energy. Often used in healing, dowsing and meditations.

ARAGONITE—a crystal with needle shaped crystals, which are helpful in times of stress and anger. Provides insight for problem solving.

ARC—a word used in areas of Scientology meaning affinity, reality, communication and understanding.

ARC BREAK—a phrase used in areas of Scientology meaning an upset with another person, group, or with the self.

ARC OF INTIMACY—in Astrology, arcs five, six, seven and eight, whose planets and signs represent lessons in love and play.

ARCANE—that which will be revealed to one when one is ready to receive it.

ARCANUM—an unknown or a spiritual mystery.

ARCANUM THE GREAT—one who had the secret which permit all magical forces to be achieved. Not yet revealed.

ARCHAEO-PROSPECTING—searching for archeological sites through the means of Dowsing.

ARCHANGEL—a superangel of the Christian and Koran beliefs. see angel.

ARCHE'—a Greek word meaning origin or beginning. Used in Metaphysical beliefs to mean Universe or Deity. The original.

ARCHETYPE—inner neuropsychic centres possessing the ability to initiate, control and mediate the common behavioural characteristics and experiences of all human beings. Primeval image or symbol.

ARIES—the zodiac sign "The Ram" March 21-April19.

ARMAGEDDON—a term used to mean the end of the world. The name of a city in Israel where, according to the Apocalypse, a battle of good and evil will take place. see apocalypse.

ARM DOWSING—dowsing by rigidly extending both arms straight out, at shoulder height. A dowsing response is indicated when one arm rises up apx. four or five inches. see one arm dowsing.

ARMS—a form of picture or art with four arms which represent the activity of male and female energies.

AROMATHERAPY—the use of the healing properties

of pure essential oils to promote the health of body and mind.

ARRIVAL KNOWING—a strong unexplainable impression that one is about to meet a specific person and then that person arrives soon after.

ARROW—a symbol of direction. In the Metaphysical belief the arrow means a 180 degree turnaround of the ego. In the Goddess belief the arrow is a divine instrument meant for both healing and death.

ART OF LIVING—developing a sense of ones life line or life plan. Treating others humanely. see life plan.

ART THERAPY—a method of helping those in a traumatic situation by having them draw their trauma, thereby helping them to deal with their situation.

ARTHUR, KING—(500 A.D.) mythical king who reigned in the times of Merlin the Great. see Merlin the Great.

ARTISTRY—a drawing, by a spiritual psychic-artist, of one's spiritual path, by using the aura as a guide. Divination by art.

ASANA—an Eastern belief system sitting position during meditation

ASCENDANT—in Astrology, the eastern horizon or location of the rising sun. The first house as a whole.

ASCENDANTALIZATION—in Astrology, the introspect made by the ascendant of one chart to any point of another chart, symbolizing the process of stylization or characterization of the affected point.

ASCENDED MASTER—one who teaches from another plane of existence by means of mediums. Direct voice messages. Dreams or visions.

ASCETIC—a non-materialistic person in pursuit of a close oneness with the universe or Deity.

ASCENSION—the belief that certain persons classified as gods, go directly to heaven after their physical death. see apotheosis.

ASCETICISM—self denial of sensory pleasures and indulgences for the purpose of spiritual growth, such as remaining celibate or fasting.

ASHRAM—a Sanskrit term for a meeting and learning place of the Eastern belief systems. A place of retreat.

ASHRAYS—a very helpful spirit or fairy originating in Scotland, very helpful in matters of complete gardening.

ASIZA—African spirits that live in the forests and grant spiritual or magical powers to humans.

ASMODEUS—king of the demons, (Hebrew Mythology) with three heads, goose feet and a snake's tail.

ASPECT—in Astrology, one of several critical geometrical angles formed between planets and angles.

ASPECT GRID—in Astronomy, a schematic graph representing all the aspects of a particular birth chart.

ASPIRANT—a person who is searching to become at onement with god or become enlightened.

ASPORT—opposite of apport. Objects which disappear into thin air, usually at seances. see apport.

ASPR—American Society for Psychical Research.

ASSOCIATION THEORY OF TELEPATHY—a theory which states that if two ideas are associated in one mind, this association may become effective in the other's mind, which is presented with one of these ideas.

ASSUMPTIOM—the act of assuming another's personality or body for the purpose of healing or helping. A form of therapy.

ASTARA—founded by Earlyne Chaney in 1951, a Metaphysical movement which believed in reincarnation based on Eastern belief, meditation and vegetarianism.

ASTON-PATTERNING HEALING TECHNIQUE—the belief that the body wants to move in an asymmetrical spiral, therefore the concept of asymmetrical movement is most important to the healing of the physical and mental body.

ASTRAL BODY—the intangible or non-material counterpart to the physical body. The non-physical facsimile of the human form which may, at will, separate itself from the actual physical body. The body of the emotions.

ASTRAL LIGHT—energy and light which vibrate at a higher rate and are not visible to the physical senses, but are very much in touch with the physical world.

ASTRAL MATERIAL—the basic substance of the fourth dimension which vibrates at a higher rate than the physical or third dimension. It is not shaped by physical forces but by thoughts and the imagination.

ASTRAL PLANE—the dimension beyond the physical world where the soul, spirit and astral body function free from the burden of the physical body, independent of the objective. The spiritual plane closest to the physical body.

ASTRAL PROJECTION—a temporary separation of the spiritual or astral body from the conscious physical body and moving about at will. see out of body experience.

ASTRAL SENSES—the belief that each physical sense has an astral counterpart which are the senses one uses when in an altered state of mind. see spiritual senses.

ASTRAL TRAVEL—the ability of the body to travel in space without the physical body, generally in the Astral plane.

ASTROLOGICAL NADIR—see Nadir.

ASTROLOGOS—the study of interconnections of objects in the universe, and how they relate and work together.

ASTROLOGY—a study of the celestial bodies and how they relate to humans. The study of planetary influences. Using the sun, moon and stars to foretell and foresee the future.

ASTRONOMY—the genuine science which developed from Astrology. see Astrology.

ASTROMANCY—prophecy or divination by using the star's movement on a daily basis. (not astrology)

ATEN—a Rosicrucian belief for the symbol of the "sole ever-living God", an objective symbol of the creative mind and divine essence of God.

AT THE READY—the position which a Dowser holds his Dowsing objects when ready to begin a dowsing search.

ATHAME—the knife used by witches to trace out the Magic Circle used for invoking spirits.

ATLANTIANS— inhabitants of the lost continent Atlantis.

ATLANTIS—the superior island which is believed to have destroyed itself by the greed of power through high technology. The creators of several mutants through experimentation of genetics.

ATMAN\ATMA—an eastern word for universal spirit, breath, ego or soul.

ATOM—the smallest division of energy matter having a complete consciousness that can exist alone,or in combination with other atoms or molecules. Part of the whole.

ATOMIC PLANE—the highest of the seven planes which psychics have divided the solar system into, each plane has seven "atomic subplanes." see atomic subplane.

ATOMIC SUBPLANE—the matter of the solar system is divided by the occultists into seven planes, the highest which is the atomic plane. Each of the planes is divided into seven sub planes, of which the highest is called the atomic subplane. see atomic plane.

AT-ONE-MENT—one's becoming or joining with the universe or Deity . Occurs in most religious, mystical and metaphysical practices.

ATRIUM—a Latin word meaning the origin or entrance. The beginning of a ritual or practice.

ATTUNEMENT—the act of being in touch with, or on the same vibrational level, as the Deity and all humankind.

AUGUR—an official diviner of Ancient Rome. To foretell the future with the use of omens. see Augury.

AUGURY—general term for all forms of prophecy. Divination based on the outcome of chance events. A form of divination using the flight and death of birds as the Auger's focal point. see Augur.

AUGUST MOON—known as the Harvest Moon. This is the month that one harvests all that has been planted. see Harvest Moon.

AUM—a sound or chant believed to center ones energy. One of Eckinkar's most used chants.

AURA—an energy believed to surround all animate and inanimate objects. Believed to be caused by mental and physical magnetic forces. Many sensitive people are able to tell the present condition of one's physical and spiritual condition by studying one's Aura. A field of multi-coloured radiations emanating from the physical body or object. Sometimes confused with a halo.

AURA HEALING—one who applies remedial colours to the Aura where a colour deficiency exists, or contrasting colours where there is an excess of one specific colour. This healing takes place by the use of visualization.

AURA BALANCING—a method of extracting negative energies from ones chakras and aura with a pendulum type object. A form of polarity healing. see polarity.

AURA IMPRINT—the affect that the aura of any object, or person, leaves on contact with any other object or person. A mixing of energies, emotions and mental states of two objects or persons.

AURAL FORCE—the energy force which emanates or radiates from any object or person, the first impression feeling. see first impression feeling.

AURAMETER—a Dowsing device with a single handle joined to a flexible wire, coiled at the center point and a small weight at the tip, used to evaluate aura's. This device is also able to detect thought forms.

AURIC EGG—another name given for the causal body. see causal body.

AUTOGENETICS—the use of basic scientific principles to create perfect health in human and animal life. Similar to self hypnosis.

AUTOMATIC SPEAKING—a phenomenon in which a person speaks without being consciously aware of what is being said.

AUTOMATIC WRITING— writing while under the control of a spiritual being. i.e. having paper and pencil in place and one's hand begins to write without the efforts of the physical body.

AUTOMATISM—physical actions which are not controlled by the conscious intelligence of the one making them. i.e. automatic writing or automatic drawing.

AUTOMATIST—a person who practices automatism. see automatism.

AUTOSCOPE—any mechanical means by which communications from the Deity or the unknown may reach us, such as the ouija board or divining rod.

AUTOSCOPY—an art in which one sees one's own physical body and inner organs from a point outside the body. see out of body experience.

AVATAR—a highly evolved spirit being who adopts a physical body so that s\he may help humans in times of great need. Avatars are difficult to identify, even by sensitives.

AVATARA—female version of Avatar.

AVEBURY—the oldest and largest megalithic site in Britain. Larger than Stonehenge. (2600-1600 B.C.)

AVIDA—a non-belief in new age belief systems. A belief that when we die nothing remains. The end of existence.

AWARENESS—the state of being informed. Transcending time and space. Being at-one-ment. The subjective aspect of reality.

AWE—something so beautiful and spectacular which puts one's mind and spirit in a beautiful state of being.

AXIS—the neutral position of a hanging pendulum during a search, from which all motions are related.

AYURVEDIC HEALING—an ancient North American Indian science of life, whose purpose is to allow one to understand one's constitutional make-up. To choose the diet and living condition best suited to one's particular needs.

AZTECS—native people of North and South America who's society rivalled that of Egypt, India and China, who believed very strongly on life after death, and that being sacrificed to the Gods was an honour.

AZURITE—a blue stone or crystal known as the stone of heaven, which stimulates the pursuit of the inner self. It enhances the opening of the third eye which in turn enhances psychic experiences.

BABINGTONITE—green to black-brown plate-like crystals used during regressions or rebirthing.

BACH FLOWER REMEDIES—Edward Bach believed that all disease was caused by moods, he used flowers and buds to treat moods, thus he treated the disease.

BACKSTER, CLEVE—a lie detector expert who hooked up household plants to lie detectors and came to the conclusion that plants can communicate with each other, can read the minds of humans and have the same emotions and feelings as humans.

BAHA'I—an Islamic cultural belief which claims that during this present lifetime spiritual destiny will be fulfilled.

BALL LIGHTING—an orange-yellow ball of electricity not often seen. Scientists have not yet been able to explain its precise nature. The balls range in size from 1 inch to 5 feet.

BANDZAWE—an African Tribe whose spiritual ancestors perform a directional divination ritual. A tribe which lives by spiritual direction believed to be that of their forefathers.

BAPTISIM—A ritual in the Christian belief representing rebirth, which is believed to cleanse the soul.

BARITE—crystals with a variety of colours used in the healing of the earth.

BARNACLE CRYSTAL—a large crystal with a group of smaller crystals growing out of its side, used to reassemble thoughts, friends, family or lost spiritual beliefs.

BASALT—a black rock which provides strength to carry on through difficult times.

Basalt also provides solidity in one's life.

BASIC TECHNIQUE—(Rhine) a form of clairvoyance testing technique using cards, where each card is held and laid aside by the experimenter as it is called by the subject.

BASISLISK—a belief of the Ancients, a legendary beast, half cock-half reptile.

BAT—many meanings. A Greek belief that if one received the bone of a bat, without killing it, one would have good luck. Chinese belief of good fortune and happiness in the presence of a bat. Christians believe the bat to be of the evil entities.

BATHING—a ritual of purification.

B.C.E.—before common era.The non religious equivalent of B.C.

BEAN-TIGHE—ghost-like spirits which appear as little old-fashioned women who are pudgy and wrinkled, originating in Ireland who choose a friendly home and watch over it, protecting it from all evil or wrongdoings.

BEAR—in most Native beliefs, the bear is the strength of the tribe. The Goddess Belief holds the Bear as sacred to Artemis (Diana).

BEAVERITE—yellowish minerals and crystals which provide communicative skills when in a difficult com municative situation.

BE—the existence of the moment, the now.

BEE—Ancient Greeks believed the bees were the souls of coming humans. The Goddess Belief called bee's "the servant's of the Great Goddess."

BEELZEBUB—Ancient belief on demons. Lord of the Flies.

BEFORE TOUCHING—(Rhine) a form of clairvoyance testing technique using cards in which a card is called before it is touched by anyone.

BEING—the abstract existence underlying all things and persons. That which is real in contrast to illusions, appearances, visions and dreams.

BELIEF—the conviction of the truth of a statement. The reality of some being or phenomenon, especially when based on examination and evidence.

BELLY CHAKRA—an energy point located in the middle of the belly. colour-orange, stone-carnelian, tone-re.

BELOMANCY—the art of foretelling the future or divination with the use of arrows.

BENITOITE—mineral or crystals with a large range of colours used to enhance contact with extra-terrestrials.

BERLINITE—minerals and crystals ranging in colour from gray to pink used to aid in the practice of patience.

BERMUDA TRIANGLE—a mysterious area in the Atlantic ocean where paranormal events have been reported to have occurred. Metaphysicians believe this to be related to Atlantis. see Atlantis.

BERTRANDITE—pale yellow minerals and crystals used to help one through all avenues of physical and spiritual change.

BERYLLONITE—white to yellow crystals and minerals which aid in fatigue.

BERZELITE—orange-yellow crystals and minerals which aid in the personal needs of intuition, sexuality and emotions.

BESANT, ANNIE—one of the main precursors of the Nu-Age Metaphysical movement. Born in London in 1847.

BEZOAR—a reddish stone found in the entrails of animals used as a powerful amulet to protect against poison.

BHAGAVAD GITA—the book used to learn the pathway to God through the Eastern belief systems. The Hindu equivalent of the Bible.

BHAKTI YOGA—the Yoga of universal love which requires nothing in return. The path of devotion through the heart. see hatha yoga.

BIBLE—the book upon which the Christian religion is based. A collection of stories, history and remberances which give the progression of God. Believed by some to be divinely inspired.

BIBLE KEY DOWSING—a Christian Bible with a key placed in it's center with the keylock part protruding. This method had been used in the sixteenth century to dowse for an indication of innocence or guilt of persons.

BIG BANG—the beginning of our evolutionary process. The beginning of our present expanding universe which happened fifteen billion years ago. The beginning of space and time.

BIGFOOT— a creature comparable to the Abominable Snowman of Tibet which lives in the forests and wastelands of North America.

BILLET READING—a test in which the tester writes a question on a piece of paper and seals it in an envelope, the reader then answers the question through paranormal means.

BILOCATION—the apparent appearance of a person in two places at the same time. It is believed that this is a learned art, rather than a gift of Metaphysics.

BIMINI ROAD—a pattern of natural rock found under

water off the coast of Bimini, believed to be built on the lost Island of Atlantis.

BIOCLIMATOLOGY—the study of the effect of atmospheric changes on the human body, very important in meditation and mediumship.

BIOELECTRICAL ENERGY—the natural energy produced in one's body by natural muscular contraction.

BIOENERGY—a power source where the energy comes from living things or persons. i.e. emotional energy, frenzied religious chanting, and healing circles.

BIOENERGENETIC EXERCISES—based on the premise that the body stores all that happens to it which may create blockages. Bioenergenetic exercises are designed to open blocked or tensed areas of the body, as the body opens, so do the feelings and emotions.

BIOFEEDBACK—a technique for helping a person develop control of unconscious, internal, biological functions with the monitoring of electronic instruments.

BIOLOCATION—the experience of being in two different locations at the same time. see out of body experience.

BIOLOGICAL COMMUNICATION—the belief that biological organisms can transmit and receive information carried on the waves of unidentified wave lengths.

BIOLOGICAL PHENOMENON—the unexplained quick and large growth of plants.

BIOPLASMA—a combination or mixture of electrons and photons creating an energy counterpart of the physical body.

BIORHYTHMS—a charting or plotting of the physi

cal 23 day cycle, the creative and emotional 28 day cycle and the intellectual 33 day cycle. One can take full advantage of the individual energy patterns in one's daily life if one knows how the physical body will respond.

BIRCH—a tree where the branches produce the best responce when used for water or mineral dowsing. Birch is also used for making Witch's brooms used in ceremonies.

BIRD—in mythology, birds were believed to carry the souls of dead persons into the next world. Accepted by most beliefs and cultures as a symbol of the soul.

BIRTH—when the soul, spirit or entity takes on the physical body and then leaves the mothers body.

BIRTHCHART—in Astrology, a map of the heaven's as seen at the date and time of one's birth, from the viewpoint of his or her birthplace.

BISMUTH—red crystals used to help one move from the physical to the astral planes. An aid to "planes" travel.

BIT—a binary unit of information used in testing telepathy.

BITYITE—yellowish crystals and minerals used to calm and maintain agility in one's life, excellent as a "pick-me-upper."

BIXYBYITE—black minerals or crystals used in the maintenance of pain throughout the body, helps with headaches.

BLACK MAGIC—a belief that one is able to invoke supernatural powers with the help of demons to harm another. Supernatural skills used to evil ends.

BLACK MASS—a ritual parody of Christian Mass performed by diabolists, where a woman's body (a virgin) is used in place of an alter.

BLACK STREAMS—underground streams which emit noxious rays that have an adverse effects on the health of those that are close to them. A dowser, witch or medium are able to change these underground energies or rays.

BLACK SUN—symbolizes many underworld Gods.

BLEED THROUGH—when one reality intermixes with another, such as hearing moans or sounds at old accident scenes.

BLIND ORE—deposits of underground ore which do not respond to any scientific equipment, only to be found by psychics or dowsers.

BLISS—spiritual awareness accompanied with a feeling of joy, contentment and peace. see happiness.

BLOOD—many cultures and religions believe that any liquid taken in ritual to be the blood of their Deity. The Goddess belief held their menstrual blood to be a sign of their creativity and fertility.

BLOODSTONE—green minerals and crystals with flecks of red which are an intense healing stone. Often called the true stone of courage.

BLUE BOOK—a privately published directory of names and information of potential wealthy sitters, secretly subscribed to by quack spiritual mediums. see sitters

BLUE LIGHT—(energy) light or colour of the throat chakra. The colour of the light waves on which communications travel. The protective healing light which is one of the light energies used to move an object towards oneself when practising telekinesis.

BODHISATTVA—those who are in need of one more incarnation to become perfect Buddha's. see Buddha.

BODILY INACTIVITY—a length of time the body is inactive as in the sleep state. When the spirit leaves the body for short periods of time.

BODY CONSCIOUSNESS—the consciousness that remains in each atom or molecule when the consciousness or soul leaves, as in the sleep state. The combined "simple consciousness'" create the body consciousness or body overseer. see simple consciousness

BODY WORK—refers to a number of Metaphysical techniques which manipulate the physical body to create spiritual alignment.

BODY WRAP—a form of healing that includes the use of herbs and heat, then being wrapped in a cocoon of sheets, towels and blankets.

BOJI STONE—used to align all of the spiritual bodies and cleanse the chakras.

BOOTHITE—light blue crystals and minerals used to help in choices. Sometimes called the guardian angel stone.

BORDERLINE STATE OF CONSCIOUSNESS—that state of mind when one is between the objective and subjective states of consciousness. i.e. pre-sleep.

BORN AGAIN— the belief that one must be baptized and learn a truth to the pathway of God. In most cases this is generally a new truth as opposed to the truth with which one was born.

BOTRYOGEN—lustrous orange crystals and minerals used to stimulate and cleanse the belly or intellectual chakra. see chakra.

BOTTLE ROD—an instrument used in Dowsing where

two small sticks are stuck into a small bottle and used as a witness chamber. see witness chamber.

BOW DEVICES—(Dowsing) a thin piece of metal, apx. ten inches long held at the ends by each hand creating a "U" shape, the dowsing reaction changes the "U" into a "Loop" shape.

BOX—(pandora's box) believed to be the container of all evil. The subconscious mind is referred to as Pandora's box, as many fear to look into it.

BRAHMA—Hindu philosophy holds Brahma as the ultimate reality. The Indo-Ayran belief is that Brahma was the medium to God. (as are Jesus and Buddha.)

BRAIN—the physical organ of the mind and physical body which controls the automatic functions of the physical body, which in turn is controlled by the soul or spirit.

BRAIN WAVE FREQUENCIES—science has knowledge of four brain wave frequencies 1-Alpha, 2-Beta, 3-Theta, 4-Delta. Each frequency has a different spiritual function.

BRAZILIANITE—yellow to yellow-green crystals and minerals used to help in the stimulation of the third chakra. see third chakra.

BREAST—symbol of femininity and life giving energy.

BREATH OF LIFE—that which is the vital life force combined with consciousness. The spirit life force.

BRIDGE—a link between heaven and earth, man and woman, conscious and subconscious, science and metaphysical. The joining of two objects, entities etc.

BRIDGE CRYSTALS—a crystal with another crystal growing into it, half in and half out of the larger crystal, used in bridging all area's of one's life.

BRIDLE—symbol of having control, of being in charge of the event or emotion.

BROADCASTING—transmitting or sending mental energy to one at a distance. A form of mental telepathy.

BROKEN TECHNIQUE—(Soal) a form of clairvoyance-testing technique by using cards where each card is lifted off of the deck of cards by the experimenter as the percipient makes the guess.

BROTHERHOOD OF GOD—advanced spirits of the deity who stand nearby and help those who want to learn and grow spiritually.

BROTHERS OF THE SHADOW—those who choose to commit themselves to negativity and negative actions .

BROXA—a witch or demon of medieval times that could change shape or form and foretell the future, it flew at night and drank blood like a vampire.

BRUSH POINTER—an artist's paintbrush made of natural fibre and suspended on a cord. Used in map dowsing. see map dowsing.

BUDDHA—(566-486 B.C.) the medium through which members of the Buddist belief speak and worship their God. i.e.Buddha is to Buddisim as Christ is to Christianity.

BUDDHISM—founded by Gautamn Buddha in the sixth century B.C. The belief that Buddha is God, or must be believed on to reach God.

BULL—the sign of Taurus in Astrology. In Tarot, the bull is assigned to the suit of Pentacles indicating they are of the element earth. The Goddess belief believes the bull to be a symbol of the

Great Mother where the horns symbolize the Crescent Moon.

BUNYIP—an Australian roaring, hairy monster known for jumping out of the water and scaring those passing by. Believed to be an omen of luck. Very helpful in assisting one who is fishing.

BUTTERFLY—symbol of change or the immortality of the soul. Of the element air. The Greek word "psyche" means both soul and butterfly, some believe the butterfly to be the souls of the dead.

BT—clairvoyance-testing techniques identified variously as basic technique, broken technique and before touching technique.

C

CABBALISTIC DOWSING ROD—(Kabbalistic) the directions for making a dowsing rod found in the Cabbala (Kabbala) are: look for a young peach, olive or walnut tree that has not yet borne fruit, grown naturally and not planted by man, must be cut just before dawn, cut a fifteen to twenty inch forked branch. While cutting, the "Cabalistic dowsing rod rite" must be spoken. Leave the rod in a Cabbala circle for twenty four hours, then break two small pieces off of the blade which cut the rod, rub the pieces on lodestone and embed a piece into each end of the rod, then recite this incantation, "by the omnipotence of Aldonay and his sons I direct thee to attract what ever I demand."

CABALISTIC DOWSING ROD RITE—as in the Cabbala or Kabbala:

"I cut thee in the name of Eloina, Miraton, Aldonay and Semiplaras, whom I plead to bestow upon thee the magic qualities and virtues possessed by the rods of Jacob, Moses and Aaron, and to impart unto thee the gift and the power to reveal that which is hidden."

CABINET—a curtain enclosed space in which mediums, conducting a seance, condense the psychic energy necessary for seance-room manifestations.

CADUCEUS—an esoteric wand entwined with two snakes, topped by a winged helmet. Used in the ancient Egyptian mystical initiations.

CAFARSITE—yellow-brown crystals and minerals used to promote group bondage. Decreases judgment.

CALAVERITE—slightly yellow shaded white crystals and minerals which help in the promotion of clear, new thought before action. Helps in the elimination of compulsiveness.

CALCITE—white crystals and minerals used to enhance the memory, both physical and spiritual.

CALL— a telepathy undertaking or test where the symbol is selected by the percipient when s\he attempts to guess a target or item.

CAMOUFLAGE—the physical reality is often referred to as a camouflage. i.e. human body, trees and tables.

CANCER—the Zodiac sign of "the crab" June21-July22.

CAPNOMANCY—The art of foreseeing the future, divination with the use of smoke from sacrificial fires.

CAPPELENITE—green-brown crystals and minerals used to balance the right\left brains and the female\male energies.

CAPRICORN—the Zodiac sign of "the goat" (December 22-January 19)

CARDINAL—in Astrology, one of the three modes of signs which are activity, initiatory and determinative. The cardinal signs are Aries, Cancer Libra and Capricorn.

CARRIER BEAM—an overground line of energy between two geometric points believed to be the beams on which psychic messages travel.

CARTOMANCY—the art of foretelling the future. Divination with the use of cards.

CASTRATION—symbolizes a loss of all male energies as well as victory over all sexual and physical desires.

CAT—indicates the loving and sinister aspects of Venus. Many beliefs hold a black cat as a negative sign, especially if one crosses one's path. The Egyptians believe the cat to be the animal which is the closest to the human consciousness with supernatural powers. Associated with witchcraft. The Goddess Diana's companion.

CATALEPSY—a state of coma and rigidity in which the normal bodily functions are suspended, generally produced in the astral body during the process of leaving the physical body. Can be self induced or an unconscious event.

CAT'S EYE—(tiger's eye) a mineral which represents luck, happiness and serenity.

CATHARSIS—cleansing oneself by relieving pent-up or negative feelings or events by expressing them.

CATHARSIS EXPERIENCE—the empty feeling which remains after a healing of releasing negatives, or negative energy, has been completed.

CATALYST—an object, entity or substance that facilitates spiritual change but does not participate in it.

CATHARS—a spiritual group of the twelfth century which believed the universe consisted of two co-existing Dieties. The kingdom of the good god with happy angels and the kingdom of the bad god with Satan.

CATLINITE—red-pink, clay-like mineral used to remember the mystics and rituals of ancient times.

CAUSAL BODY—neither a subjective or objective body, but the center of the ego consciousness, this spiritual body remains throughout all the incarnations. The soul or higher self.

CAUSE—one's daily actions. The day to day actions which help create one's reality, as in cause and effect. see effect.

CAVE—many meanings. Symbol of the womb. Security of home. Birth-channel.

CAYCE-EDGAR—(1877-1945) an American psychic known for his trance readings of illnesses and remedies. The sleeping Prophet.
C.E.—before common era the non religious equivalent of A.D.
CELESTIAL—of the sky or heavenly bodies. A physical or spiritual entity in the networking of the universe. Referring to heaven or the divinity.
CELESTIAL BEING—a heavenly or mythical being. A spiritual being known to be on earth for the purpose of helping humankind during spiritual growth.
CELESTIAL SANCTUM—a universal meeting place of all the highly advanced souls or spirits. A Universal place from which radiates all the positive energies needed for good health, kind thoughts, love and healing.
CELL—a fundamental form of all creation, having a wall of negative polarity and a nucleus of positive polarity. A combination of both the physical and spiritual energies.
CELTIC—(1739) members of the early Indo-European peoples who came from the British Isles and Spain and settled in Asia Minor. Believed to be highly versed in the spiritual mysteries.
CENOBITE—members of spiritual groups living together in a monastic community for the purpose of spiritual growth.
CENTAUR— half man, half horse creature originating from Greek mythology.
CENTER—believed to be the location of all divine knowledge existing in the physical body. Only attainable through meditation and spiritual assistance. All things have a center.

CENTRE OF TRANSMUTATION—power houses, or places of great power, where negativity is transformed into positivity which is assisted by the Ancients or Adepts of Shamballa. see Shamballa.

CEREBRUM—the most recently evolved portion of the brain which is responsible for higher mental and spiritual functions.

CHAINS—symbol of restraint, slavery or loss of freedom. Also a symbol that one must restrain ones physical actions and emotions.

CHAITYA—another term for the long dormant Mid-Aura Chakra.

CHAKRA—(ALSO CHALKRA)— the energy centres that link the soul to the physical body. Each Chakra has it's own colour, musical note, healing stone and day. Although chakras are open at birth, they continually mature and are more active/receptive with age. All charkas are located on the spine. The rainbow shows the true order and colour of the chakras.

CHAKRA FIXATION—a time during a spiritual plateau when one is not ready to move upward to the next spiritual step. see fixation.

CHAIN—many beliefs interprete this to mean a self imposed restriction.

CHALCEDONY—a stone with a wide range of colours used in the promotion of stability within group ritual or meditation.

CHALDAEANS—an Ancient Babylonian people who wrote "The Chaldaean Oracles". A book which was later regarded, by the Neo-Platonists, as a sacred book known for its magical and religious practices.

CHALICE—a cup in which fluid, representing the blood of Christ, is used in rituals.

CHAN—a Japanese word meaning meditation.

CHANCE—the unpredictable element of existence pertaining to both physical and spiritual realities.

CHANNELLED WRITING—receiving information from another mind, the universe or any deity as it is being written or documented.

CHANNELLING—one who is a medium to the spiritual world. The transmission of information or advice to people in this reality from spirit guides in another reality.

CHANTING—songs or chants differ in most beliefs. Some forms are: using the vowels, om, aum and hu. A ritual that is believed to heal, condition chakra's and re-energize the body.

CHANTWAYS—many American Indians have been known to carry on chanting for days thus finding the pathways or chantways of spiritual energy.

CHARGE—to spiritually empower an object with energies by the use of visualization or meditative requests.

CHARIOT—The Qabilistic writings hold the chariot as a symbol of the human body. This was also the belief of Carl Jung. The one who holds the reins and the animal pulling the chariot determine it's positivivity or negativity.

CHARLATAN—one who is a fraud in all areas of existence. Pretending to be or know something which one does not know. False prophet. False channeller.

CHATOYANCY—the phenomenon of movement, illumination or opalescence found within a stone, such as tigers eye, fire opals and moonstone. Ancients believed stones had souls.

CHEIROMANCY—the art of foretelling the past, present or future by using the palm. Palm reading.

CHELA—a Buddist student.

CHELATION—receiving certain substances intravenously for the purpose of cleansing the blood. Believed to be inspired by God which is not yet proven as no one has claimed this treatment.

CHI—Chinese word for life's breath force or energy. Prana in Eastern and Indian beliefs.

CHI SPIRITS—spirits of pure energy originating in China believed to assist with maintaining good health.

CHIASTOLITE—stone with a large range of colours which has a "cross" of contrasting colour within it, used to avert the curse of the "evil eye." see evil eye.

CHILD—symbol of growth yet required. Symbol of the future and mysteries yet to be experienced. Jung called the child a protective force coming from the subconscious.

CHILD MEDIUM—children who have the gift of mediumship. They are very lonely children so they choose spirit children as playmates. see spirit children.

CHILDRENITE—yellow or brown crystals used to control the temper.

CHINESE WRITING ROCK—a rock with crystals grouped like "Chinese writing" used to assist in receiving information from the Ancients and the Akashic records.

CHOCOLATE MARBLES—petrified mud balls used to eliminate worries, stress and anger. Used to promote happiness.

CHOHAN—an adept who has reached the levels of Lord, Master or Chief.

CHOSEN ONES—the first spiritual teachers to come to earth, chosen by the Appointed Assembly. see appointed assembly.

CHRIST—the medium in the Christian belief. Jesus Christ is God to those of the Christian Belief.

CHRIST CONSCIOUSNESS—a concept of oneness with God. When one acknowledges the Christ light, one acknowledges the oneness of the Deity or God.

CHRISTIAN SCIENCE—a Christian belief that a human is a spiritual being made in the image of God. They do not believe in evil or suffering of sins. They believe that all healings come from God. Founded by Mary Baker Eddy (1821-1910).

CHRISTIAN SPIRITUALISTS—spiritualists who stand by the bible, following the leadership and knowledge of Jesus Christ.

CHRISTIANITY—a belief that Christ is God, or that one must believe on Christ to get to God.

CHRISTOLOGY—study of the theories of the meanings of the Christian belief and Jesus Christ. Most Christologies are focused on the New Testament.

CHROMOTHERAPY—a method of healing with colours. Each chakra has its own colour which corresponds to that part of the physical body.

CHURCH OF ALL WORLDS—a belief inspired by Maslow's self-realization theory, aided in the growth of neo-pagan and witchcraft religions.

CHRYSOBERYL—crystals and minerals with a wide range of colours which increase physical and spiritual powers.

CHURCH OF LATTER DAY SAINTS—(Mormonism) founded by Joseph

Smith Jr. (1805-1844). It is believed that the angel Moroni delivered plates written in Egyptain-like hieroglyphics to Smith which were later translated. This belief has some resemblance to the Metaphysical Beliefs.

CHURCH OF SCIENTOLOGY—founded by Hubbard in 1953. One of the basic theories of Scientology is to overcome negative effects of the present and previous lives.

CHURCH OF TZADDI—the goal of this church is to educate its members in spirituality, ancient wisdom and science. Founded in 1962 by Amy Kees in Orange County, California.

CINNABAR—vermilion-red to brown-red crystals and minerals which promote one's knowledge of business and financial affairs.

CIRCLE—continuation of the soul. Never ending existence. Eternity. Jung holds the symbol of the circle to mean the ultimate state of oneness. see healing circle.

CIRCULAR DOWSING ROD—a rigid wire or tubing which can be bent into an open or closed circle, held in the prominent hand, chest high, the reaction is the same as the Y-Rod.

CITRINE—yellow to golden-brown crystals and minerals used to balance the yin-yang energies. see yin-yang.

CLAIRAUDIENCE—to hear beyond the normal physical sense. A Metaphysical belief of an inner voice coming from the universe, spiritual guide or god. This practice is used for telling the future, helping solve problems and relationships.

CLAIRSENTIENCE—a gift of identifying objects, people and health problems through the feeling of the inner body and mind provided by the universe, spiritual guides or Dieties.

CLAIRVOYANCE—to see beyond ordinary time and space. Awareness or response to objects or events without the use of the physical senses. The great gift of seeing events in the inner mind, provided by the universe, spirit guides or Dieties. This practice is used in various helping situations.

CLAIRVOYANT—one who is gifted with clairvoyance. see clairvoyance.

CLAIRVOYANT DOWSING—seeing the required targets such as gold, water and health in the mind's eye.

CLAW OF THE DRAGON—an Ancient Chinese term for a geological irrigation zone, an area where underground rays or energies are irritating to humankind. see energy changers.

CLERIC DOWSERS—another term for priests who practice exorcism.

CLEROMANCY—the art of foreseeing the future by casting lots.

CLEVER MEN—Australian term for aborigines with psychic powers. Believed to be twenty percent of the Aboriginal population.

CLOUD DISSOLVING—a feat of psychokinesis in which clouds are made to disappear or dissolve by concentration of thought and will.

CLOUDS—symbolize a short time of discomfort. Many Chinese beliefs have the cloud symbolizing the female, and rain symbolizing the male.

CLOVER—the symbol from which all "trinity " beliefs were to have evolved, the Christian Trinity, The Triple Goddess and the Three Mothers of the Celts.

COBALTITE—silver-white crystals and minerals used to develop one's creativity.

COBRA—symbol of the kundalini force of the chakra's. See kundalini.

COGNITION—a term covering all modes of conscious knowing.

COLD MOON—December 21-January 19. Named after the coldest month of the year.

COLEMANITE—milk-white crystals and minerals used to develop one's survival skills, both physical and spiritual.

COLLECTIVE UNCONSCIOUS—a term introduced by C. Jung to designate those aspects of the psyche which are common to all mankind.

COLOR—the Metaphysical belief that colors transmitted psychically or physically can assist in the healing and growth of specific situations. The meaning of colors may differ with different beliefs

COLOR HUNGER—one who is deficient in one or more colors of the cosmic spectrum of light. A need for sunlight.

COLORED QUARTZ—different colored quartz crystals used for specific healings. Chakra colors. see individual colors. see chakra.

COLUMN—a symbol of the phallus. Pairs of columns symbolize the balance or duality of all things. The Goddess Ceres held the column as a symbol of love.

COMMUNICATOR—a personality stating to be that of a deceased person which communicates with the living, usually through a medium.

COMMUNIGRAPH—an instrument for communicating with the spirits. A table with a small pendulum underneath it which lights up the alphabet written on the top of the table as delivered by the spirits.

COMPLEX OUT OF BODY EXPERIENCE—when the complete soul or vehicle of vitality leaves the physical body, as in death or the delta level of sleeping. see simple out of body experience.

COMPOSITE CHART—in Astrology, a synthetic chart that symbolizes the spirit of a particular human partnership, based on the midpoints of the individual birthpoints.

CONCENTRATION—an emptying or quieting of the mind, then focusing one's attention towards the "center" of one's being. A state necessary for meditation, stillness is also required for meditation.

CONCEPT—a mental understanding of some event or aspect of reality. see conception.

CONCEPTION—one's concept, or understanding, is dependent on one's beliefs and knowledge. see concept.

CONCRETION—a small mass of cemented minerals with small hollows which have pebbles inside. Believed to have magical powers and used in spiritual ritual.

CONCURRENCE—the theory or way in which the Deity allows, but yet is not the cause of, human actions. Free will or choice.

CONE OF POWER—a force field of psychic energy raised by a coven of Witches for magical purposes.

CONJUNCTION—in Astronomy, an aspect characterized by a zero-degree separation between two planets, symbolizing the process of fusion or collision. see Orb.

CONSCIENCE—moral sense of knowing one's actions which create right or wrong. The mind or knowing of the conscious self. Knowing all truths, all laws and all principles.Feeling good about one's actions. Spiritual awareness.

CONSCIOUS MIND—the analytical, materially based rational half of the mind as opposed to the passive spiritual half.

CONSCIOUSNESS—a way of perceiving the various dimensions of reality. Our day to day means of understanding our actions.

CONSCIOUSNESS OF WHOLENESS—each element of life is both a wholeness within itself and a creative contributor to some greater whole of which it is a part. Understanding the realm of the spirit.

CONSENSUS REALITY—the accepted view of reality within a particular culture, the spiritual view reinforced by cultural institutions.

CONSTELLATION—a group of stars named after the figure which the stars are thought to form. Used in astrology.

CONTACT TREATMENTS—when one giving a healing treatment physically touches the one treated. Physical contact during a spiritual treatment.

CONTAGIOUS MAGIC—the continued influence upon each other of objects that have previously been in contact with each other.

CONTINUITY OF CONSCIOUSNESS—an uninterrupted psychic search of one's past, present and future lives.

CONTRACT—see healer's pact.

CONTROL—the primary spirit with who a medium works. The spirit regulating which other disembodied entities may speak.

CONTROL SERIES—a form of telepathy test under strict laboratory conditions.

CO-ORDINATE POINTS—channels through which energy flows as warps and invisible paths from one reality to another. They also act as transformers and provide much of the generating energy that makes creation continuous. These points are and attract pure energy that propel what is not yet physical into the physical.

COPAL—an Aztec incense made of pitch.

COPPER—copper-red mineral used to promote self-esteem, independence and success.

CORAL—a wide range of colors, an underwater mineral used to stimulate psychic phenomenon.

CORE BELIEF—beliefs one was raised with, learned from parents and society.

CORER MUTANTS—descendants of the scientists and miners who learned to live underground when trapped in tunnels or caverns. They are believed to be sixteen feet tall.

CORNETITE—blue-green crystals and minerals used to enhance the acceptance of the dual nature of all things.

CORNUCOPIA—symbol of plenty. A symbol of maternal and phallic importance in the Goddess belief.

CORPORUM MUTATIO IN BESTIAS—the belief that through negative or black psychic powers one is able to change into the form of an animal such as the werewolf. see werewolf.

COSMIC—a state of condition of cosmic order and regulation. The universe seen as a harmonious relation of all natural and spiritual laws. The intelligent universe.

COSMIC CONSCIOUSNESS—total knowledge of the universe past, present or future as it is at this moment. A Metaphysical belief that one knows all and all knows one. The energy of the Deity which creates and pervades all space. A sense of unity with the Universe.

COSMIC EGG—according to Ancient Egyptian ritual, the whole of the universe is an egg conceived in the creative time of the Gods.

COSMIC METABOLISM—the overall multidimensional realities in which each reality or spiritual level exists and pulsates. The total cosmic, reality, level or existence of networking. see pulsating consciousness.

COSMIC MIND—referring to the total mind or intelligence which creates cosmic consciousness. see cosmic consciousness.

COSMIC PICTURE GALLERY—a scenic representation of every thought, feeling and action since the beginning of time. see Akashic records

COSMOGONY—a study or theory of the physical and spiritual creation, or origin of the world or universe.

COSMOLOGY—a scientific study of the philosophy of the complete universe.

COSMOS—a system of worlds and beings all governed by the same laws and order.

COTTINGLEY FAIRIES—(1917) two small girls of Bradford, England had taken pictures of fairies (possibly made of paper) and produced them as real, which were accepted as truth until 1945. Doubt arouse from the British Society for Psychical Research. There is doubt today about the authenticity of these fairies.

COUNCIL OF THE ELDERS—elevated Dagon spiritual beings who are concerned and responsible with all aspects of meditation. The ones who give direction through one's meditation. see Dagon .

COURSE IN MIRACLES—a self study spiritual growth course that was channelled through an atheist over a period of seven years. It is non-denominational but takes many teachings from several beliefs such as Christian, Zen and the Vedas. A spiritual way of life channelled by Helen Schucman from 1965 to1972. The course consists of 3 volumes totalling apx. 1100 pages.

COVELLITE—indigo-blue crystals and minerals used for caution in communications, especially to recognize and correct verbal error.

COVEN—a group of witches (thirteen) gathering to practice their skills.

COVENANT OF THE GODDESS—box 1226, Berkeley, California 94704. Founded in 1975.

COW—held in a high spiritual position in the East Indian belief. The life giving and sustaining power of creation. The female version of the Hindu God Brahma. The Norse Goddess Audhumla was believed to be a cow and licked the first being into a living being.

CRANE—(Bird) Chinese symbol of justice and the good soul.

CREATE—to bring into existence through Spiritual means or thoughts.

CREATION—the activity of the personal creator, from a point in the infinite past, which brought this physical world into being out of thought form.

CREATION SPIRITUALITY—Matthew Fox began a movement in 1960's to redefine and revitalize Christianity. One of his elements of change was the use of mysticism.

CREATIVE VISUALIZATION—the repetitive use of mental imagery to achieve desired goals in life.

CREATOR—one who creates. see create.

CREMATION—burning of the physical body after one dies. The Ancients believed this to be the appropriate method of dealing with the physical body after one had died or passed on.

CRESCENT MOON—the figure of the moon at such a state defined by a convex and a concave edge symbolizing movement between dual energies. Strong Goddess beliefs and meanings.

CRIMEN EXCEPTUM—the legal status of the crimes ascribed to the witch was extraordinary, allowing procedures not allowed in other "normal" crimes. Witch crimes were treated as secular since they were thought to be directed against humans and God.

CRISIS APPARATION—an apparition seen at or about the time one is going through an unexpected crisis.

CROCODILE—an Ancient Egyptain symbol for evil and fury, also devious knowledge.

CROMLECH—a circle of prehistoric stones. The symbol of the great Mother Goddess with the opening co-insiding with that of her birth channel.

CROMAAT—an Ancient Egyptain word translated to mean "as in truth", quite frequently used in upper class rituals of Egyptain based beliefs.

CRONE—the mature, wise and knowledgeable aspect of the Goddess trinity.

CROP CIRCLES—areas where crops have grown to heights of apx. ten feet high overnight with no explanation other than some external force was responsible. Over 100 crop circles were found in England between 1980 and 1987.

CROSS—many meanings. Pre-Christian symbol of fertility in the joining of man and woman. That which Jesus died upon in the Christian belief. A crossing of oneself. The symbol of the trinity. see Ankh.

CROSS CHECK— a form of mental telepathy testing which ensures ESP is taking place and not the physical mind. Two mediums receiving the same messages at the same time.

CROSS CORRESPONDENCES— communications conveyed by two or more Mediums at the same time but not in the same place. The individual communications may seem nonsense, but are thought to be significant when combined with each others.

CROSSING OVER—the leaving of our physical body and once again becoming pure spirit. What we, in the western world, call death.

CROSSROADS—Carl Jung called it a joining of opposites. A mother symbol of the Goddess belief.

CROW—many meanings. Symbol of the creation of the daylight hours.Great civilizer. Mystic powers of foresight. Spiritual strength found through the Crone aspect. A symbol of the Celtic Goddess Morrigan.

CROWN—a symbol of a great spiritual achievement. The Egyptain crown showed the Cobra of the Kundalini energy. see kundalini.

CROWN CHAKRA—the energy center at the top of the head, color-white, flower-lily, stone-diamond, tone-te, gland-pituitary.

CRUCIFEX—a Christian amulet in the form of a Latin cross, often with the figure of Jesus on it.

CRYOLITE—wide range of colors, these crystals and minerals are used to enhance public speaking.

CRYPTESTHESIA—an old term used to mean ESP, coined by Richet.

CRYPTOGRAPHY—a form of writing which the Ancient spiritual people used to maintain secrecy in their writings. Writing in an ancient code.

CRYPTOMNESIA—memories not available to the five senses. Deja vu, a possible explanation of memories of past lives. The use of altered states of mind to return to past lives. A form of hypnosis or regression.

CRYSTAL—a mineral believed to have healing, magical and divine powers.

CRYSTAL BALL—a ball made of clear crystal used in crystal gazing. see crystal gazing.

CRYSTAL GAZING—one who uses a crystal as a focal point when foretelling the future rather than cards or runes. see scrying.

CRYSTALOGRAPHY—the scientific and spiritual study of the many minerals classified as crystals.

CRYSTAL MERGING—a thought process for attuning one to their own personal crystal. A visualization that one enters their crystal and creates a common vibration, thus giving one the power of the crystal.

CRYSTAL WOMAN—a Mayan Goddess which is the transmitter or message carrier between Spiritual persons and humans. A word used for a medium in Belize.

CUBANITE—a brass to bronze colored mineral which is highly magnetic, used to attract those one wishes to attract to oneself.

CUCUI—a spirit of Mexico used to discipline children through fear, telling the children that if they are not good the Cucui will get them.

CULT—a group of people or branch of a belief system which is completely made up of one person's beliefs. These beliefs may be very positive or negative.

CULT OF DIONYSUS—a following of the Mythological god of wine Dionysus, (Baccus) who's doctrine was that the madness of excess wine drinking was a spiritual gift.

CULTURE SHOCK—in Astrology, a type of composite chart of two people, that is very different from either person's birth chart, indicating that they both need to make major adjustments if they choose to remain in contact with each other.

CUMBERLANDISM—the act of divination by watching the subtle movement of the muscles. see muscle reading.

CUPBEARER—a symbol of a message recieved from God or the diety which is of a positive nature.

CUPS—in Tarot, a symbol of knowledge, perception, love, pleasure and enjoyment. One of the four suits in the Tarot deck.

CUPPING—a method of applying heat and healing directly to the body. A heated glass is placed on the body creating a vacuum. It is left on the body for apx. fifteen minutes. This is believed to suck or vacuum out the pains of illnesses such as arthritis or muscle pain.

CUPRITE—deep red crystals and minerals used to alleviate worries which are beyond one's control.

CURSE—a prayer or invocation for harm to come upon another. To bring evil upon another person.

CURSE OF PRINCESS AMEN-RA — a curse of an Egyptian Princess laid to rest 1500 years before Christ. Bad luck would come to anyone who disturbed her. A story in the early 1900's states that four Englishman bought the mummy of her, since then all have had bad luck or died.

CURTAIN—symbolizes a door between the two worlds of the physical and spiritual realities.

CURVED CRYSTAL—an unnatural but rare crystal with a definite curve in it's body. Used for healing energy bodies such as the aura, etheric and astral bodies.

CUSP—in Astrology, the beginning of a house, an unclear zone extending about a degree and a half on either side of the beginning of the house. A point of change.

CYBERNETIC—the use of feedback in control and communications.

CYCLES—the ancients divided time into cycles of various duration's, from a second to an infinite number of years. Cycles mark events in the worlds physical, mental and spiritual happenings. A regular sequence of recurring events.

CYCLOPS—symbol of uncontrolled or unpredictable emotions causing tunnel vision. A Mythological being with one eye.

CYPRESS TREE—
ancient mythology believed this tree to be a sacred tree of emotion. Now dedicated to the planet Venus and the Goddess.

D

DACTYLOMANCY—a form of self-made ouija board using a ring on a string and a board with the letters of the alphabet on it. When a question is asked the ring held above the board will spell out the answer.

DAGON—an Atlantean Race who were introduced by the Chosen Ones. see Chosen ones.

DALAI LAMA—religious and temporal leader of Tibet, meaning oceans of wisdom.

DAMPENED REACTION TIMES—Dowsing reactions which are sluggish, inaccurate or completely absent. Factors which cause dampened reactions are stormy weather, extreme heat, ones physical or mental fatigue or improper friction or positioning of the used dowsing object.

DAMSONITE—a violet colored stone with yellow designs flowing throughout. Used to stimulate all aspects of femininity.

DANALITE—a wide range of colored crystals used to promote self cleansing. Helps to eliminate one's troubles.

DANCING—used in rituals for releasing unwanted emotions, energy and feelings for another person. Many believe dancing pleases their God.

DAPHNITE—deep green colored crystals and minerals used to promote communication with the plant world.

DARKNESS—a symbol of things turned in the wrong direction. Sadness. Unpredictable actions. Lack of spiritual understanding.

DATA—information received and recorded from physical or spiritual beings.

DATOLITE—a mineral used to help gain respect from those around one.

DAUGHTERS OF GOD—the Koran refers to the three Pagan Goddesses, Lat, Uzza and Manat.

DAY OF THE DEAD—an Ancient international yearly holiday in which the dead are honoured by various practices such as dancing, feasting and fasting. The modern day Halloween was a Day of the Dead. A day where the living and the dead come together to celebrate.

DEATH—the shedding of the physical body. When the physical body has completed its reason for being in this lifetime. Passing over to the spiritual world. The greatest psychical experience.

DEATHBED VISIONS —paranormal experiences of persons dying, such as visions of the dead, religious figures or people previously passed over, these visions support the theory of consciousness after death.

DECAPITATION—a Celtic belief that the spirit resided in the head, hence the preservation of the heads. Separation of the physical from the spiritual.

DECEMBER MOON—known by many cultures as the Cold Moon as this is the coldest month of the year in most areas. see Cold Moon.

DECLINE EFFECT— the tendency of one who initially performs well to show a decline in spiritual performance over a period of time.

DEER—symbol of simplicity, love and kindness. A mystical experience in the future.

DEJA VU—the feeling and illusion of having previously experienced something actually being experienced for the first time.

DELIRIUM—an altered state of consciousness characterized by irrational thought and behaviour brought on by various conditions including fear of the spiritual unknown.

DELTA—a level of sleeping where dreams occur.

DELUGE—usually referred to as Noah's flood. Destruction followed by new life.

DELUSION—a spiritual belief that has no bases for truth.

DEMATERIALIZE—to disappear from the vision of the human eye. To be without physical molecules. To disappear.

DEMOCRACY—in Astrology this is a type of composite chart which contains elements reminiscent of both people in a relationship, indicating that they are compatible and both will have a voice in the relationship.

DEMON—many meanings in different beliefs. Christians believe demons are devils or Satan. Greeks believed demons to be minigods. Demon in Greek means "replete with wisdom". One's negative thinking. One's own creation. An ancient Greek word, Daimon, meaning spirit which was usually meant to represent an evil force.

DEMONOLATRY—the worship of demons or devils.

DEMONOLOGY—a specialist in the study of demons or devils.

DEMONOPATHY—behavior of a person interpreted to be that of a person under attack of a negative energy or demon. see demon.

DEMONSTRATION—the process of producing one's thoughts into the physical world dependent upon understanding and application of spiritual principles.

DENDRITIC CRYSTAL—a quartz crystal containing a branching figure within itself resembling moss or a small branch.

DEPOSSESSION—the releasing or exorcism of discarnate spirits attached to humans.

DERMOGRAPHY—writing on ones skin not produced by external physical means, a form of stigmata. see stigmata.

DERMO-OPTICAL PERCEPTION—the study and ability to determine brightness and color through the sense of touch. see skin vision.

DERVISH—a Moslem mystic, ascetic holy one. A Moslem belief which specializes in ecstatic practices.

DESCENDANT—in Astrology, the most western horizon or the sign on it. The seventh house as a whole.

DESCENT—the shift of consciousness from outside the physical body to inside the body. Returning after astral travelling. The soul entering the fetus apx. two months before birth or at birth.

DESERT—symbol of the Hebrews meaning, those having the correct religion.

DETERMINISM— the belief that each event is predetermined by past events, thus present events determine future events.

DEVA—a Sanskrit word meaning shining one or god. A celestial being.

DEVAS—a spirit originating from Persia which shows itself as a golden-yellow shinning light. Believed to be helpful in sending extra energy, when asked, to all rituals.

DEVELOPMENT—one who is on one's spiritual journey and is progressing towards the understanding of the universe, or deity, and its existence.

DEVIL—many meanings. A creation of one's own psyche. Evil forces and events.

Negative thoughts. Negative energy.

DEVOUT—an Eastern term meaning one who follows his chosen belief.

DEW—symbol of messages sent from the Divinities.

DHARMA—a Sanskrit word meaning law of nature. Spiritual code of behaviour.

DIABANTITE—a dark green colored mineral, used to help end personal situations such as relationships, friendships and professional relationships.

DIAKKA—a term formed by Dr. Andrew Davis to mean undeveloped, ignorant, mischievous and evil spirits.

DIAMETRIC HYPOTHESIS—a possibility of Psi to achieve in one act, rather than a step by step process, what seems to require more than one act of Psi. see psi.

DIAMOND—wide range of colored crystals and minerals which are known as the king or queen of the crystals. Used to enhance all powers known to humankind.

DIANETICS—the searching, finding and most often the erasure of engrams. (negative pictures, energies, etc.) A belief that most spiritual or psychological problems stem from traumas experienced in the womb before birth or past lives.

DIDA OBI—the Kola nut divination system in Nigeria.

DIETY—one's supreme being—God, Universe, Jesus or Buddha.

DILOGGUN—a seashell divination system in Nigeria and other African countries.

DIOPSIDE—wide range of colored crystals and minerals used to enhance mathematical intelligence.

DIRECT—in Astronomy, the normal forward motion of a planet through the different astrological signs of the zodiac.

DIRECT-VOICE COMMUNICATIONS—a spirit communicating directly to a person or a group of persons, without the use of human vocal chords, often using musical instruments.

DISCARNATE ENTITY—a being or spirit without a physical body.

DISCIPLE—one who follows a teacher or master for the purpose of learning to teach and live according to his\her teachings.

DISCARNATE—a spirit in energy form. Pure energy. Spirit without a physical body.

DISEASE—a general disturbance of the constructive process of the living cells believed to be brought on by one's mental state. Lack of spiritual belief.

DISEMBODIED— the learned art of separating the spiritual body from the physical body and remaining in control of that body.

DISHABITUATION— heightened sensitivity of the physical body due to the presence of new stimulation, as in spiritual growth or awareness.

DISK—Chinese symbol meaning the sun and heavens. A winged disk means moving from physical to spiritual.

DISTAFF—a symbol of the Fates meaning continuing creation. The female branch of the family. see fates.

DISASSOCIATION—the breaking of a strong bond to which one was associated, necessary for healing.

DIVINATION—the process of discovering future or past events, and gaining unknown information through unconscious or supernatural means.

DIVINE—of the universe, god or great spirit.Beliefs pertaining to these superior beings.

DIVINE CATASTROPHE—a Kabbalistic term for the time when the sparks of divine light fell to the earth and were trapped in matter. see Kaballa.

DIVINE INTELLIGENCE—same as cosmic consciousness or god consciousness.

DIVINE MIND—the consciousness of the Deity which pervades all. (universal mind, cosmic mind, god mind)

DIVINE PLAN—the plan from the universe or deity pertaining to the complete outlook of this and other realities. The original plan for the human race.

DIVINER—one who tells the future, seeks out objects etc. through the use of uncommon practices.

DIVINING ROD—an instrument used by a dowser such as a twig, wires, bones and springs. see dowser.

DIVINITY—another word for God, Ancients, Spiritual Masters, etc.

DIXON, JEANE—well known for her prediction of President Kennedy's assignation in 1963.

DOG—an Ancients belief that the dog had a very high spiritual consciousness, therefore became one's helper and best friend.

DOGMA—a set of plans or rules expected to be followed. Generally pertaining to religions rather than Metaphysical Beliefs.

DOGMATIC—one who believes in strong spiritual or religious teachings rather than experience. see ritualistic.

DO-IN HEALING EXERCISES—re-introduced to North America in 1968, these are a form of healing exercises similar to yoga. These exercises stimulate both the physical and spiritual bodies.

DOLOMITE—wide range of colored crystals and minerals used to relieve sorrow, and to make one understand that everything happens for a reason.

DOLPHIN—symbol of spiritual prudence and speed. Believed to be one of the closest animals to human thinking and spirituality.

DOOR—symbol of entrance, generally into the future and a new spiritual experience. see cromlech.

DOPPELGANGER— a German word meaning the ghost or aberrational double of oneself.

DOUBLE—an apparition of a living person believed to be a projection of the astral body. Signifies the duality of all creation. see wraith.

DOUBLE TERMINAL CRYSTAL—a crystal with both ends having a six sided head or point.

DOUBLE WHEEL—An Ancient Chinese belief that the double wheel meant infinity, showing the eternal circles of life on earth, surrounded by the larger circles of the cosmic universe.

DOVE—many beliefs have the dove as a symbol of peace, friendship, love and a messenger from God. Connected with the Maiden aspect of the Goddess.

DOWSER—a sensitive person who has the psychic ability to locate minerals, water and mining locations by using dowsing rods. Dowsers also have healing abilities.

DOWSING—searching for items such as water, metals and entities through psychic means. Usually using a form of dowsing rod.

DOWSING CHART—any list or design which is constructed for use with a dowsing instrument. A diagram with answers to one's specific questions where a pendulem is used.

DOWSING REACTION—when the dowsing rods find their target by either dipping, vibrating or bobbing over the required object.

DOWSING RODS—many types, the basic types of rods are angle, y, or straight rods. Generally made of willows, birch or clothes hangers.

DRAGON—symbolic figure found throughout the world with many contradictory meanings such as fear, strength, fire and hades.

DRAGON'S BLOOD—see cinnabar.

DRAWING DOWN THE MOON— a Wiccan ceremony held on or near Dec 12, dedicated to Bacchus, the God of wine and fertility.

DREAM—regarded as an occult science. A visual experience during the sleeping hours. Dreams represent one of the most extraordinary mysteries of life.

DREAM BODY—similar to the astral body. It is believed that sensitives are able to transfer their consciousness to the dream body to understand and study everything that transpires during sleep.

DREAM TIGER—a psychic animal who controls or is responsible for one's dreams, especially when answers are needed.

DREAMING TRUE—a state of having control and consciousness in the dream state.

DREAMS—Dreams occur in the Delta state of mind when one is a asleep. Dreams can be futuristic, present or past experiences relived, warnings, problem solvers, prophecy, guidance etc.

DROP-IN COMMUNICATORS—an unknown or uncalled for entity that drops in at a seance, generally with a specific message for one of the members from a specific entity.

DRUGS—the use of drugs to enter an altered state most often has negative results. Artificial entry to an altered state of mind.

DRUIDS—a priest, healer or medicine man of the ancient Celts. Modern Druids have developed many of the Ancients practices and have added new mystical rituals of their own.

DRUM—believed by the Shamans that the drum helps one enter the subconscious mind or altered states of mind.

DRYADS—tree dwelling spirits from Celtic countries, mainly female, which teach the secrets of the Divinity, very playful.

DUFTITE—light to dark green colored crystals and minerals used to increase one's physical and spiritual attention span.

DUMONTITE—yellow crystals and minerals used to enhance one's imagination.

DWARF—symbol of the keeper of the gate between the conscious and subconscious minds.

E

EAGLE—a symbol of all seeing, all knowing power. Overseer. Freedom of spirit. Associated with power and war.

EAR OF CORN— Often associated with the Earth Mother.

EARTH—the reality where souls inhabiting the physical body have chosen to have their physical experience. In Astrology, one of the four elements, earth symbolizes patience, practicality, realism and stability.

EARTH ACUPUNCTURE—pounding large nails or stakes into the earth's surface to reduce or neutralize harmful rays or energies as in black streams. see black streams.

EARTH-BOUND SPIRITS—when one dies or passes on and the soul cannot let go of the earth-life identities, loved ones or possessions. A form of a ghost.

EARTH FORCE—a term for a theoretical telluric force emanating from the surface of the earth, one of the energy forces used by psychics, mediums and dowsers.

EARTH MIND—thinking and development that does not expand beyond the thinking of man on the planet Earth.

EARTH'S POLAR CHAKRA—energy of the earth's north and south poles believed to be the major life line of the earth.

EARTH SIGNS—the astrological Earth signs are Taurus, Virgo and Capricorn.

ECKANKAR—a movement founded in 1965 by Paul Twitchell believed to be a secret path to the deity. Eckankar believes in the ancient science of soul travel aided by living or passed over masters.

ECLIPTIC—in Astrology, the apparent path of the sun, moon and planets against the stars; the zodiac.

ECSTASY—a state of intense or extreme joy as in self-realization. A change in the center of perception from the material to the spiritual world.

ECTENIC FORCE—another term for psychic force or energy. see psychic energy.

ECTOPLASM—a substance held to produce spirit materialization, a white substance emanating from a mediums body creating a likeness of the self. see ideoplasm.

EFFECT—the result after an action has been taken, as in cause and effect.

EGG—symbol of the birth of creation. Immortality.

EGO—the state of self-interest, the part of the personality which one consciously refers to as the "I".

EGO BOUND—held in spiritual rigidity with the intuitive portions of the self either denied or distorted beyond any recognition.

EGOIC GROUPS—the mental bodies which are the expression of the ego are found on the third subplane of the fifth plane. see plane.

EIDETIC MEMORY—remembering by seeing something mentally exactly as it was in the physical reality.

EIGHT—many meanings. Material progress and health. Good judgment. Justice in all things. Completing the old to make room for the new.

ELECTROENCEPHALOGRAPH-(EEG)—a piece of scientific equipment for recording brain waves.

ELDERS—psychics hold elders to belong to a spiritual council who plan the future's course. Other beliefs hold the elders to be wise, intelligent spiritual persons.

see council of Elders.

ELECTRON—a basic form into which spirit energy concentrates in preparation for physical manifestation.

ELECTROMAGNETIC REALITY—when emotions, thoughts or ideas are still in their own simple spiritual form without physical bodies.

ELECTRUM—the blending of various metals such as gold and silver. Rarely found in nature, the resulting metal has a long magical history.

ELEDAA'—the equivalent to a guardian angel in most African belief bystems.

ELEMENTS—earth, air, fire, water, the building blocks of the universe. The four fundamental psychic processes of consciousness. see akasha.

ELEMENTALS—beings or objects from other planets. i.e. extra terrestrials. Spirits of the elements fire, air, earth and water. Nature forces. Some believe elementals to be a lower form of spirit.

ELEPHANT—symbol of strength and power in India as well as many other cultures.

ELESTIAL CRYSTAL—an etched or layered crystal used in transformations of energy, emotions and health.

ELEUSINIAN MYSTERIES—the classical period of ancient Greece produced a mystery religion in which members were sworn to secrecy. The doctrine was to have a better fate in the afterlife. The principle Deities were Demeter and Persephone who was the wife of Hades, ruler of the underworld. There are no clear records to date.

ELIAT STONE—blue and green crystals and minerals used to promote growth towards wisdom.

ELIXIR OF LIFE—a liquid sought by the Alchemists because it was thought to cure illnesses and confer eternal youth.

ELLIPSE—the Egyptians believed this to be a symbol of the superconscious.

ELVES—international spirits which appear in the "dress"of the land in which they exist. They are willing to help but must be asked before doing so.

EMANATIONS—radiations or projections from all physical or psychic form, extensions of the vibrations within the form. After death energies that remain in the physical reality which sensitives are able to feel.

EMBOLITE—yellow to green colored crystals and minerals used to purify the aura.

EMERALD—emerald green crystals and minerals used to enhance domestic bliss. Known as the stone of contented love.

E-METER—a portable electric device used in Scientology about the size of a cigar box. Used for gauging one's mental state and it's moment to moment changes. The E-meter is based on a Wheatstone bridge (which measures differential resistance in an electrical current) and has dials, knobs, and needles with two empty tin cans clamped to wires connected to the box which are gripped by the patient during an auditing session.

EMMANUEL—the identity of the voice channelled by Pat Rodegast who wrote the book "Emmanuels Book: A Manual for Living Comfortably in the Cosmos." A Metaphysical Book.

EMOTIONS—a psychic and physical reaction subjectively experienced as strong feelings and physiologically involving changes that prepare the body for immediate vigorous action.

EMOTIONS OF BEING—subtle emotions that often accompany the quiet-mind experience of existence such as peace, quiet, joy, happiness and the good fortune of others.

EMOTIONS OF REACTION—non-spiritual unpleasant states of mind which arise in reaction to certain stimuli. Some of which are desire of others, greed, lust, envy, jealousy, anger and hate.

EMOTIONAL CONTAGION—the sudden mutual joy and excitement of a feeling that can occur in a group that is exposed to the same emotional arousal.

EMPIRICISM—the belief that all of ones knowledge is derived from experience, thus the purpose of continual reincarnation.

EMPTYING ONESELF—the process of clearing the mind of thoughts and personal ego in order to allow the flow of Universal or God's energy and thoughts. Preparation for meditation.

ENDOSOMATIC—pertaining to the inner or spiritual body. see exosomatic.

ENERGY—having the capacity of action or of being active. That which creates power.

ENERGY ANCHOR—applying spiritual energy after a healing and instructing that energy to remain until the healing is complete.

ENERGY BALL—golf sized balls of energy used by psychics to massage one's body, usually left on through the night.

ENERGY CENTRES—see chakra's. Seven major centers of the physical body that receive and send energy. In most cases the glands.

Hindu belief has eight chakras.

ENERGY CHARGERS—one who has the ability to charge or endow objects with spiritual or protective energy as in crystals, amulets and talisman.

ENERGY COCOON—an cocoon type "energy ball" left on a patient after a healing to ensure a complete recovery. Usually left on until the healing is complete. see energy ball.

ENERGY DIRECTOR—another term for one who uses spiritual energy for the purpose of healing. Spiritual healer. see healer.

ENERGY PERSONALITY ESSENCE—a spiritual entity no longer focused in physical form. see incarnate.

ENERGY POINT—a point in a residence, location or event where the spiritual energy is the strongest which is percieved by psychics.

ENERGY TRANSFER—moving spiritual energies from one person to another, as in a healing. see healing.

ENGRAM—the unconscious residue of a past experience that exercises a harmful influence over the present. A sudden trauma caused by shock. An altered state of mind assumed to result from the excitation of certain stimuli. A mental state or picture containing pain or discomfort.

ENHYDRO—a mineral which contains fluid used to understand the feelings of others.

ENOCHIAN—a language of the angels which has a syntax but is very cumbersome, used to communicate to sensitives.

ENTITY—an invisible being or spirit without the physical body.

ENVIRONMENTS—primarily mental creations of

consciousness, thrust out in many forms.

EPHEMERIS—a book on Astrology listing the positions of the planets each day at a certain time over a long period of time.

EPIPHANY—the appearance of a god or goddess on earth in human form.

EQUANIMITY—freedom from the need to act, do or change what is happening at the present moment. A spiritual peaceful state.

ERDLUITLE—spirits originating from Switzerland, very helpful in controlling the weather to assist farmers with their crops. When they shift to the physical reality they have webbed feet which are needed when they walk about the fields.

ESCHATOLOGY—the study of the end of time or the end of the world as we know it and the fate of the individual soul. The study of reincarnation.

ESOTERIC—refers to spiritual experiences relating to the inner or God spirit of the physical body.

ESP—knowing something without the use of the five physical senses. see extra sensory perception.

ESSENCE—that which makes a thing what it is. The inner nature of all reality. The most important portion or quality of a person or object.

ESSENES—members of a Jewish sect who lived in the Dead Sea area before and after the birth of Christ. The discoverers of the Dead Sea Scrolls.

ESSENTIAL OILS—fragrant, volatile substances produced by certain plants. The "blood" or life force of the plant. Used in the art of Aromatherapy.

ETERNALIZATION—the infinite goal or objective which one sets with the help of the brotherhood. Results of the trinity, God, Man and Thought.

ETERNAL TRUTHS—truths that have been with us since the beginning of time such as the sun rises in the morning.

ETHER—the space or state between energy and matter. A spiritual energy. see etheric body.

ETHEREAL MAN—the belief that man has to experience an etheric type body before entering the physical body, pre-existing physical reality.

ETHERIC BODY—the vehicle through which flow the streams of vitality which keep the physical body alive. A ghost-like body or energy which is found surrounding all things. One of the major bodies of the Metaphysical Belief. The link between the soul and the body.

ETHERIC SURGERY—surgery performed on the etheric body with the help of spiritual guides. This is believed to be the body upon which the psychic surgeons of the Philippines operate.

ETHICS—a system for measuring one's moral, spiritual or mental state of mind at any given moment. A set of rules by which one lives or conducts oneself.

EUCHROITE—emerald green crystals and minerals used to build satisfaction with oneself and never to be alone again.

EVANGELISM—Christian method of spreading their word. Preaching the Christian word.

EVANSITE—wide range of colored crystals and minerals which assist in seeing the truth even though one is in a confusing situation.

EVEITE—apple green crystals and minerals used to assist one to be in a state of readiness at all times, called the stone of readiness.

EVIL—the concept of evil is believed to be the absence of God or the Deity. Negative energy. Deliberate wrong doing with the intent to harm.

EVIL EYE—a belief that some practitioners of the supernatural can kill or bewitch with a simple look. This can be done either consciously or unconsciously. In many cultures the wearing of an ornamental eye is thought to avert this evil spell. see psychic attack.

EVOLUTION—the belief that one evolves from a lower form as one grows spiritually. From plant, to animal, to human. see big bang.

EVOLVED—one who has completed ones life plan through reincarnating many times and has reached perfection. God-like.

EVOLUTIONARY HISTORY—an inner record of all changing patterns of one's lifetimes and incarnations from the beginning of one's mental pattern.

EXCESS ENERGY—see sudden excess energy.

EXIST—to have real being either material or spiritual. To have being in space and time. An occurance.

EXISTANCE—reality as opposed to appearance. Reality as presented in experience. The state or fact of being.

EXISTENT—the realm of the phenomenon in which manifestation occurs. The state of being now. Being or existing at this instant.

EXISTENTIALISM—a 20th century philosophical movement which stresses the active role of the will rather than of reason when confronting problems posed by a hostile universe without knowledge of right or wrong.

EXISTENTIALIST—one who follows the doctrine of existentialism.

EXORCISM—the driving out, or expulsion, of unwanted spirits by means of spiritual rituals.

EXOSOMATIC—pertaining to the outside or physical part of the body. see endosomatic.

EXTERIORIZATION—the state of being out of one's body, out of body experience.

EXTRA-TERRESTREAL INCARNATIONS—a theory of reincarnation that one may incarnate into different forms, even as beings from other planets or demigods. see extra-terrestrials.

EXTRA-TERRESTRIAL WALK-INS—an extra-terrestrial spirit which occupies a physical body that has been vacated by it's first or original soul. see walk-in and extra-terrestrial.

EXTRA-TERRESTRIALS—beings from anywhere but the planet Earth. Beings from outer space.

EYE—associated with the sun and/or moon in ancient Egypt. Judgment by the Dieties.

EYE OF HORUS—an Egyptian amulet bearing the eye of the falcon headed solar and sky god.

F

FAIRIES—(Faery) mythical beings of folklore and romance usually having diminutive human form and magical powers. see Cottingly fairies.

FAIRYISM—having the power to enchant.

FAIRY-LAND—the land of the fairies. A place of beauty and magical charm.

FAIRY-RING—the folklore belief that such circles or rings were the dancing places of Fairies. Mushrooms found in the forest growing in a circle.

FAIRY-TALE—(1749)an event, story or adventure involving unnatural forces such as fairies, goblins and wizards.

FAIRY-TALE—(1820)story or fable marked by unusual beauty and grace.

FAITH—many meanings. That which does not require a belief. A simple knowing. An active belief.

FAITH HEALING—the curing of an illness by a simple expression of faith that one will be healed. Praying at the four points of the body, forehead, two shoulder points and the base of the spine. (the christian cross)

FAMILIAR—a spirit, ghost or demon which obeys a shaman, medicine man or witch when regularly called upon.

FAMILY KARMA—groups of people who reincarnate together as families to reap or correct the effects of past interactions.

FAN—symbol of femininity, intuition and change. Phases of the moon.

FAQUIRS or FAKIR—a Moslem or Hindu holy man who mortifies his flesh in order to control it. Wonder-workers of the East, not always spiritual, but with knowledge gained by family transmission.

FARADAY CAGE—a metal room or cage designed to prevent the transmission of electromagnetic waves used in ESP testing.

FARSIGHT—another term for clairvoyance. Seeing into the future.

FATA—Goddess of Fate.

FATHER—symbol of the male principles of creation. The conscious mind.

FATHERHOOD OF GOD—the belief that people come from the same source. Particularizations of abstract beings.

FATIGUE EFFECT—a fatigue which begins when more than twenty minutes of Metaphysical work has taken place. When one becomes a little "off" with their work. A short rest is required to continue.

FAUNA—a belief that all animal life has spirits. Animal wisdom. see flora.

FAUSTITE—apple green crystals and minerals used to help one appreciate the outdoors and all of nature.

FEATHER—(plume) Egyptian symbol of faith, truth and contemplation. Element of Air.

FEATHERED MEDICINE STICK—the North American Indian's Dowsing instrument.

FEBRUARY MOON—known as Snow Moon because of the sparkling beauty of the snow. see Snow Moon.

FECES—many cultures hold the vision or appearance of feces as a symbol of riches, purity and gold. A form of reverse symbology.

FEEDBACK—conformation of the results of a given test or action.

FELLOWSHIP OF THE HEALING LIGHT—a society founded by the channeller, Paul Solomon, whose work is very much like that of Edgar Casey. A community has developed from this society called "Carmel In The Valley" located in New Market, Virginia.

FENG SHUI—a Chinese art of physical placement. A placement of ones furniture has much to do with energy flow in the home, a placement of clothes on the body has much to do with how one feels, etc.

FERRIERITE—white crystals and minerals used to help keep one in a comfortable meditative state.

FERSMANNITE—dark brown crystals and minerals used to help in the stimulation of the mind.

FETISH—an Egyptian object worn to represent spirits for protection, love and repelling evil.

FEY—a term used in ancient Scotland describing a person who foretold the future.

FIELD—the space surrounding every object or person in which the aura's influence is felt.

FIELDS OF CROPS—symbol of unlimited potential and expansion. Earth Gods and Goddesses were connected to fields of crops in that they had the power to enforce production or non-production.

FIFTH ESSENCE—(element) many meanings. That which ties all objects, stars, suns, etc. together in the multi-universes. That which holds the parts of "all that is" together. Consciousness. Thought. In addition to the four elements of fire, earth, water and air, the Ermatic tradition believed in a "fifth essence'" sometimes called "burning water," "the soul in the spirit of wine," or "the water of life." It was a strong alcohol that made man incorruptible and renewed his youth. One way of making it was to distill wine "one thousand times." It's modern day version is "grappa."

FIFTH RAY—the ray of solid spiritual knowledge and science. see ray.

FIFTH ROOT RACE—the Aryan Root race to which the American, European and Hindu races belong. see root races.

FIGURE EIGHT LAYING ON IT'S SIDE—a symbol meaning the eternal life of all realities, such as conscious and subconscious.

FILLOWITE— yellow-brown crystals and minerals used to eliminate procrastination.

FINAL CAUSE—the final cause, reason or explanation of an entity, shows the purpose of it's intention to serve, as in choosing a path for enlightenment.

FINDHORN—spiritual community in Northern Scotland seemingly endowed with special powers.

FINITE— having limitations, not forever or ongoing.

FIRE—many meanings. In Astrology, one of the four elements, fire symbolizes the development of will. To the Chinese, symbol of the sun. Egyptians, the Sun and spiritual strength. India, symbol of destruction.

FIRE EATING—the art of putting ignited objects into one's mouth without being harmed or burned. One is most often in an altered or spiritual state of mind. see fire walking.

FIRE IMMNUITY—the ability of coming into direct contact with fire or red hot coals without being burned or harmed. There have been many reports of this phenomenon throughout history.

FIRE SIGNS—the astrological fire signs are Aries, Leo and Sagittarius.

FIRE WALKING—a form of purification. An art of walking on red hot coals without being harmed. Having the belief that one will not be harmed makes it so. see fire-eating.

FIRE WORLD—another term for the aura. see aura.

FIRST IMPRESSION—the personality impression one receives of another person when one enters anothers energy or visual field. The first impression one receives of another just by seeing that person.

FIRST IMPRESSION FEELING—the feeling one gets about another person as one moves into anothers aura field. see field.

FIRST RAY—the ray of will and power. see ray.

FIRST ROOT RACE—a now extinct Slavic language (Polabian) and people who lived on the Baltic Coast, the original spirit humans. see Polaria

FISH—many meanings. A special sign in many of the Christian religions. An idea or thought. Symbol of the subconscious. Symbol of sexuality and fertility to the great mother of the sea.

FIVE—many meanings. Uncertainty. The ability to move from one place to another without cause or warning.

FIXATION—when one is "stuck" in a particular place of one's spiritual growth. see chakra fixation.

FIXED—in Astrology, one of the three modes of the signs stability, strength of purpose or stubbornness. The fixed signs are Taurus, Leo, Scorpio and Aquarius.

FLAME—a symbol signifying the state of one's consciousness or spirit. i.e. the larger the flame the more advanced one's consciousness.

FLIGHT—symbol of the spirit or soul escaping from

the physical body thus avoiding being trapped by addictions, sensations or emotions.

FLINT—gray-colored mineral used to promote spiritual thought and thought transference.

FLOGGINGS—the belief of some cultures, "to flog one is to drive out the demons."

FLORA—a belief that all plant life has spirits. Plant wisdom. Plants. see fauna.

FLORENCITE—pink crystals and minerals used to promote spiritual work involving flower essences.

FLOTATION THERAPY—a form of therapy where one relaxes in a tub of salt water apx. 93 degrees F. This relaxation makes meditation flow smoothly.

FLOWERS—a symbol of love, desire, happiness. Each flower color signifies a different emotion. Essential oils are produced from flowers.

FLUORITE—wide range of colored crystals and minerals used to discourage disorganized or unsatisfactory spiritual growth.

FLUTE—a male and female combination where the shape is masculine and the music is feminine.

FLY—symbol for astral travel.

FLYING—associated throughout history with witches flying with or without brooms.

FLYING SAUCER—name first used for disk-like objects in the sky. The modern UFO's.

FOAM—symbol of semen arising from the ancient tale of Uranus's genitals being dropped into the sea, they created foam.

FOCAL CENTRE—the point in consciousness, mind or spirit where psychic communication begins.

FOHAT—the permanent electrical energy. The universal propelling vital force. The root of all electrical phenomenon.

FOOT—spiritual symbol of the connection to the earth. Foundation. To receive the power of the Goddess, one must stand before her in one's barefeet.

FOLK MAGIC—the practice of melding bioelectrical energy with natural, universal energy to bring about needed change.

FORD—spiritual symbol of an easy crossing to the spiritual side of reality.

FORE-SIGHT—having the spiritual gift of seeing into and knowing the future.

FOREST—spiritual symbol of life experiences past and yet to come, dependent on where one stands in the forest.

FORM—shape, style or design of any physical or spiritual body or object.

FORTEANA—an unexplainable phenomena such as floating balls of light in the night sky, apparitions, stigmata and raining frogs.

FORTUNE TELLING ACT—vagrancy act under which mediums are included. The general category of rogues and vagabonds in England which dates from the rule of King George IV. By the application of Act 5, George IV. c. 83 mediums accused of fraud, or the intent to deceive, are liable to three months imprisonment. The Witchcraft Act (9 Geo. II. c. 5) offers grounds for similar prosecution.

FOSSILS—preserved remnants of the past used as a bridge to the future, especially in psychic work such as foretelling the future or regression.

FOUNTAIN—spiritual symbol of fulfilment. Youth.

wisdom, purification.

FOUR—many meanings. Reality. Material manifestation. Spiritual understanding and acceptance. Logic and reason.

FOURMARIERITE—red colored crystals and minerals used in spiritual medicine or healing work.

FOURTH DIMENSION—that which lies beyond the three physical dimensions. Realm of mystery. The place of the universal electronic vibrations. The dimension or place of the coming together of atoms and electrons which create physical reality.

FOURTH RAY—the Ray of beauty, harmony, art and unity. see Ray.

FOURTH ROOT RACE—the Japanese and Chinese belong to the Fourth Race, see Root Race

FRAGMENT SELVES—parts of the self not yet belonging to the complete self. A need for a spiritual healing. Unmanaged and uncontrolled parts of one's emotional body.

FRANKLINITE—black colored crystals and minerals used to assist in self-preservation of the physical and emotional bodies.

FRAUD—spiritual trickery. Leading others to believe that one has abilities that one does not have.

FREE WILL—the ability to choose one's direction in all area's of one's existence.

FREUD, SIGMUND—Freud, in his private life was one of the first, along with Jung, to explore the conscious and subconscious minds.

FRIDAY—considered a lucky day to one who believed in the Ancient Deity. A day sacred to the Goddess.

FROG—many meanings. Spiritual symbol of birth. Good luck. Fertility.

FRUIT—a symbol of ancient belief signifying fertility. As you sow, so you reap.

FRUITARIANISM—a diet which limits one's diet to uncooked fruits and nuts. Believed to be followed by many Metaphysicians.

FUTURE MEMORIES—another term for precognition.

FYLGIAR—a spirit first seen in Iceland which is one's personnel spirit guide throughout one's life, seen only at death.

G

GADONG ORACLE—a Tibetan monk used as an oracle by the Tibetian Government prior to the Chinese intervention, now in exile.

GAIA HYPOTHESIS—a theory which states that all humanity is interconnected with the whole of the universe, that the totality composes but one entity or being. That humanity is the nervous system of the planet.

GAL VIHARA—carvings on a natural wall in Ceylon, two of Buddha and one of Ananda.

GALENA—black colored crystals and minerals used to enhance the centering of one's energies.

GALVANIC SKIN RESPONSE—(gsr) a method of measuring body changes caused by stress, psychic energy or tension. This is done by measuring the amount of moisture produced by the body. Also used in psycho-testing.

GANOPHYLLITE—brown-yellow crystals and minerals used to help with physical protection.

GANZFELD—a blank visual field produced artificially, used in the testing of ESP.

GARDNERIAN WITCHCRAFT—founded by G. Gardner (1884-1964) who wanted to, and organized a form of witchcraft which existed in Europe, the bases of which is living with, rather than opposing nature.

GARLIC—ancient and modern belief that this herb will protect one from witches and demons when placed above the door and from the "evil eye" when worn on one-self. see evil eye.

GARNET—wide range of colored crystals and minerals used in extracting negative energies from one's spiritual bodies. (most common color is a deep red)

GARRETT, EILEEN—(1893-1970) a gifted medium who was one of the first to encourage science to explore paranormal phenomena. Born in Ireland of Celtic beliefs.

GATES—another term for the energy chakras. Entrances to new levels of consciousness.

GELLER, URI—Israeli psychic who was known for his ability to bend spoons mentally, stop watches,and be correct in five out of six lab tests.

GEM THERAPY—the directed use of gem color and molecular energies for the enhancment and balancing of one's energy flow. Generally applied through the aura. Walking through a buried crystal field is one form of gem therapy.

GEMATRIA—a predominantly German Kabbalistic belief known and used in the 13th century, one of the Kabbalistic belief systems.

GEMINI—the Zodiac sign "the twins" May21-June20.

GEMSTONES—a belief that gemstones, as do flowers, have certain healing and helping qualities.

GENERATOR CRYSTAL—a large six sided crystal creating an apex which is free of all markings.

GENETIC—physical, mental or spiritual traits transmitted by heredity through the genes.

GENETIC MEMORY—one of the theories to explain instant past life recall by those who question reincarnation.

GEO—a prefix meaning earth or the planet earth.

GEODE—a round spiritual stone or mineral which contains a cavity lined with growing crystals projecting into the hollow, it has the power to enhance all psychic phenomenon.

GEOBIOLOGY—the study of how the earth's gravity or rays affect the physical and spiritual bodies of humankind.

GEODETIC LINES—underground energy lines to which psychics, mediums and all sensitive people respond.

GEOELECTROMAGNETIC FORCES—pertaining to the gravitational pull of the earth which sensitive people are very susceptible to and are in tune with.

GEOHYGENIC PLANNING—the placement or non-placement of buildings, roads etc. based on the results of the tulleric currents or energy fields examined by a psychic.

GEOMAGNETIC FIELDS—the magnet fields related to the natural magnetization of the earth. Psychic's are sensitive to changes in these fields.

GESP—general extrasensory perception. ESP which can be telepathy or clairvoyance or both.

GESTALT—a type of psychology treatment which requires closure. Spiritual closure. A clear picture. An integrated whole which is more than its parts.

GESTALT FLIP—the state of mind which occurs when one sees more than is presented to one, especially if one is changing states of mind as in going into alpha. see alpha.

GHOST— many meanings. A visual apparition without a material presence. Remaining spirit energy of a person recognizable as that of a deceased person or animal. The remaining energy a person leaves behind,especially if one dies unexpectedly. A spiritual appearance in the time of need. Warning. Visions of comfort.

GHOST DANCE—a dance to evoke the dead to return to the realm of the living. Founded by Jack Wilson, a Shaman, in 1890.

GHOST LIGHTS—mysterious phenomena of lights appearing around the world, mainly in remote areas, near power lines and mountain tops.

GHOUL—from Arab demonology, a one-eyed monster with wings and animal shape, having the reputation of living on dead bodies.

GIFT—special and learned talents that are God-given. i.e. clairvoyance.

GLANDS—transformers of energy. Chakras.

GLASTONBURY SCRIPTS—(1497-1534) the name of a series of nine small booklets channeled by Johannes Bryant, a Glastonbury Monk, containing automatic writings concerning the Abbey and it's history.

GLOSSOLALIA—speaking in pseudo-tongues, interpreted to be fragments of a language never learned by the user. .

GLOTTOLOGUES—mediums speaking in unknown tongues. see xenoglossis.

GLYPH—in Astrology, all of the written symbols used as a form of shorthand. A symbol or letter of writing.

GNADENZETTEL—a special writ of mercy usually issued by a prince or bishop, which grants the condemned (assumed witch) death by decapitation or strangulation before burning.

GNOMES—small entities or elementals who live beneath the surface of the earth who tend to dislike humans.

GNOSTICS—a mixture of Astrology, Kabala, Christianity and Egyptain mysticism which formed a number of sects but were banned from the Christian Church because of their unorthodox rituals.

GNOSTICISM—many meanings. A dualistic, mystical Christian religion which sprung up in the Mediterranean area during the 2nd century A.D. Often called the religion of spiritual knowledge. A belief that this world and all the persons living in it sprung up from an evil deity who had trapped souls in the physical world.

GOAT—an ancient Mythological symbol of an over indulgence of sexual matters. A term for a non-believer in Metaphysics.

GOD—that which one perceives to be greater than oneself and is dependent upon for direction. The creator of the creation. An intelligent universal energy force which oversees all of reality. see Goddess.

GOD-?????—words that follow God indicate what it is that one believes. i.e. God the father or God the judgment.

GODDESS—the female principal of the divinity. see God.

GODDESS BELIEF— the feminine aspect of the Divinity. The Goddess trinity consists of maiden, mother and crone based on the Lunar cycle of the moon. Goddess worship extends back to the Neolithic era of apx. 10,000 years ago. Some Ancients believe the Goddess may have preceded God, creating the Universe by fertilizing herself.

GOD-FORCE—the power that acts according to natural law. The power that manifests thoughts into physical objects.

GOD-MIND—that which satisfies one perfectly. That which never runs out of energy. A spiritual belief that one is comfortable with.

GOD OF THE UNIVERSE—an understanding of God which has no inhibitions or limitations to one's actions. That which is in control of the universal networking.

GOD SELF—the entity within which is connected to the supreme entity or Deity.

GOD FORCE—the power of the Deity that acts according to principle. That which manifests thoughts into the material world.

GOETHITE—wide range of colored crystals and minerals used to aid one in one's life journey. see life journey.

GOLD—a natural gold colored metal symbolizing purity and truth.Corresponds to the deity. The color of God energy. Superiority.

GOLDEN AGE—an ancient period of wonderful and magical events and accomplishments that are proven by ancient myths and beliefs. A time-period of plenty, peace, harmony and beauty.

GOLDEN FLEECE—quest of presumably the impossible. A symbol of one who tries to reach the unobtainable.

GOLEM—in Hebraic Mysticism, a monstrous automation given life through magic.

GOOSE—similar to the symbol of the cow in India. Held sacred to the Celts who did not eat this bird.

GORGON—often associated with the power of the Kundalini in a positive manner. A being from the mythological tale of Medusa.

GRACE—that which is given freely without expectation of financial return. Forgiveness. Unconditional help. The act of the deity bestowing deserved or undeserved favor upon one.

GRAIL—a point of contact with a supernatural and spiritual reality which possesses unlimited healing powers. A vessel in which the life of all humanity is held and symbolizes the body of the Goddess or the Great Mother.

GRAIN—the symbol of life. A food which sustains all life.

GRANITE—wide range of colored crystals and minerals used to assist in keeping one on track of this life-time experience.

GRAPES—an ancient belief to be the nectar of the gods. Abundance. Pleasure. Bacchus, the god of wine is often associated with grapes.

GRAPEVINES—a symbol of a continual supply of love, growth, abundance and pleasure. Blessed by Bacchus, the god of wine.

GRAPHITE—iron black colored crystals and minerals used as spiritual energy con ductors in healing by enhancing the energy sent from healer to subject.

GRAPHOLOGY—the study of character analysis based on one's handwriting.

GREAT INITIATES—see Initiates.

GREAT PYRAMID OF GIZA—believed by many psychics to have been built with mental powers which produced the inner energies which, according to psychics, are still unexplained. Believed to hold the secret records of all history, past, present and future.

GREAT WHITE BROTHERHOOD—a body of physical and spiritual beings which represent mystical and esoterical doctrines. A spiritual group with the knowledge and wisdom of many ancient spiritual minds . A belief established for the earth-born during the Lemurian Age. Rosicrucians often call themselves the great white brotherhood.

GREATER REALITY—that which creates the consciousness which creates this present reality. A complete spiritual reality.A belief that God is the greater reality.

GREATER SEVEN—those who embody life force energies of the seven rays. see seven rays.

GREEN LIGHT—(energy) the light and color of the heart chakra. Healing light travels best on the waves of green light. One of the light energies used when pulling an object toward oneself in the practise of telekinesis.

GREENOCKITE—orange colored crystals and minerals used to enhance one's drama abilities.

GREENPEACE—came into existence in 1971. A strong environmentalist movement which influenced many governments to change directions on issues of the environment.

GRIMOIRE—a witch's or warlock's textbook, originally in manuscript form, passed from generation to generation. A manual for invoking magical forces. see gromorium verum.

GROMORIUM VERUM—a magical treatise published in 1517. It described a wand made of elder or hazel, carved with magical inscriptions. see grimoire.

GROSSULAR GARNET—wide range of colored crystals and minerals which are used to assist one in legal affairs.

GROUP—a number of persons that work together and attend the same spiritual meetings or functions.

GROUP KARMA—karma from another lifetime caused by a group, this karma must be worked out by the same group.

GROUP SOUL—the theory that two or more individuals who seem distinct because they occupy separate bodies, but in fact, have one soul among them.

GROVES—sacred places of the Goddesses, especially if and where sex magic is practiced.

GROWTH—accepting and advancing along spiritual beliefs.

GROWTH PLAN—a plan devised by the soul or spirit before entering the physical body.

GUARDIAN ANGEL—a spiritual being who chooses to help one in the physical world. A protector. A teacher. A leader.

GUARDIAN SPIRITS OF THE RACES—those advanced spirits which have specific knowledge on guarding the races. see Root Races.

GUIDES—spiritual teachers. Masters or beings who are here to assist one on the physical plane. see spiritual guides.

GURU—spiritual teacher or leader. A mentor of the Eastern belief. A divine teacher of Hinduism.

GUT FEELING—another term for intuition. see intuition.

GYPSUM—wide range of colored minerals used to assist in the keeping together of one's thoughts. White is the most common color of gypsum.

GYPSY—dark Caucasoid people coming from India to Europe in the fourteenth century, using the gift of foretelling the future for a fee to maintain their existence.

GYROMANCY—the art of foreseeing the future. Divination by using the physical body of a person spinning around until he or she gets dizzy and falls.

H

HABIT—that which after many repetitions becomes natural. Automatic actions used in meditations and rituals.

HADES—referred to as the Greek god of the underworld and king of the dead. Hell.

HADITH—the spiritual sayings of the prophet Mohammed which refer to the afterlife .

HAIR—some Ancient cultures believed that women with long hair could control the elements (wind, rain, creation) by loosening or tightening the hair.

HALITE—yellow and red crystals and minerals used to aid in the control of mood swings.

HALO—a circle drawn around or above one's head to indicate divinity. The Aura or energy field around one's head. Kundalini energy rising through the head chakra.

HALLOWEEN—All Hallow's Eve first celebrated on May 1st in 610 A.D. A Christian festival moved the date to Oct 31st in 834 A.D. Originated from the times of the Druids and presided over by the Lord of Death. Now considered a harvest festival. Feared by many Christians as it is associated with witches and devils.

HALLUCINATION—a vision, apparation, ghost or other phenomenon which seems, upon examination, to have been the result of the imagination rather than paranormal event.

HAMBERBITE—white crystals and minerals used to enhance states of joy, truth and contentment for mediums when in a meditative trance.

HAND—Chinese symbol of the hand and eye combined was the sign of clairvoyant ability.

HAND OF GLORY—a pickled and dried hand cut from one who has been hanged, used in casting spells and finding treasures.

HANDS—the right hand signifies positive and masculine energy, the left hand signifies negative and feminine.

HANDS PSYCHIC CENTER—the energy center in the center of the palm or the "cup" of the palm. Used to transfer energy during a hands on healing.

HAPPINESS—our basic or root spiritual mental state. Awareness combined with joy and contentment. see bliss.

HARBIN HOT SPRINGS—Box 782 Middletown, California, 95461. A metaphysical community focusing on holistic health.

HARD-WIRED—that part of the mind which has learned unwanted habits which cannot be changed without drastic intervention.

HARE KRISHNA—a cult originated in 1948 by a Calcutta mystic. Swami Prabhupada, born Abhan Charan De in 1895. Introduced to the Western world in 1965.

HARMONIC CONVERGENCE—the idea of Jose Arguelles, who in 1983 connected astrological configurations to chronological forecasts and came up with the supposed end of the materialistic world. This was to have occurred on Aug 16 and 17, 1987. A new mentality was born, a shift from tribal consciousness to planetary consciousness, from hate to love, from conflict to cooperation. The shift is believed to be the result of the peak of a powerful cosmic force.

HARMONIUM—a sense of peace with the Universe or

Deity. Unity of thought or agreement. Kinship of souls.

HARMOTOME—wide range of colored crystals and minerals used to help one to remain on schedule.

HARP—angelic instrument. Manifestation of the will.

HARPY—mythical monster grasping unscrupulous persons associated with the underworld. Goddesses working with Neptune who were the bearers of punishment.

HARVEST MOON—September 22-October 22. This was the month to harvest all that one had planted. A time to harvest all natural healing herbs and vegetables for the winter months.

HATHA YOGAA— a form of breathing exercises and sustained body postures which cleanse the physical body. see bakti yoga.

HAUNTINGS—the appearance or manifestations of ghosts and apperations in specific places.Uusually a dead person that had significant role in the life of the person being haunted.

HAWK—Egyptain symbol of the soul, the vehicle of transportation.

HEAD—many cultures believe the head to be the dwelling place of the soul.

HEADACHE—symbol of one who is unable to face reality. Problems.

HEALER—one who has learned, or has been given special knowledge and abilities on the use of healing eneries.

HEALER'S PACT—a pact that a spiritual healer has with the universe or God. i.e. if the healings are incorrect, will harm a person or interfere with one's karma, then the healing should not take place.

HEALING—receiving universal energies for the purpose of regenerating all cells of the physical body.

Receiving a spiritual blessing from the Diety. Energies channeled to a person.

HEARING FONDLE— a Psychic with the ability to touch and listen to an inanimate object from which he or she receives information.

HEART—a symbol of the positive thoughts, emotions and feelings. The organ which the Egyptians left in the mummies

HEART CHAKRA—the energy center of the heart area. color-emerald green, stone-emerald, tone-fa.

HEARTH—symbol of comfort. Love of home.

HEAVEN—Peace within oneself, heaven within-heaven without. A self-made state of mind and body. Ancients believed there was more than one heaven. A Christian belief that if one does good to oneself and others throughout their lives, their final reward will be a wonderful place called Heaven.

HECATE—the daughter of Perseus and Titan. The patron Goddess of Witchcraft. Ancient Greek Goddess of women, often portrayed as the moon.

HE-GOAT—associated with Pan. Uncontrolled sexual need. see Pan.

HEINRICHITE—yellow to green crystals and minerals used to promote the bonding of a relationship.

HEIROPHANT—one who has the knowledge to understand uninterpreted documents. Teachers of the mysteries. The highest adepts in antiquity. see adept.

HELL—intangible home of evil spirits, condemned spirits and the residing place of the devil. The deep areas of the subconscious with areas which have not yet been addressed. Christians believe that if one is evil or does harm to others, they will go to this uncomfortable place called hell.

HEMATITE—a metallic-gray luster mineral which enhances the ability of the physical mind to receive spiritual information.

HEMISPHERE—a portion or part of the whole. In Astrology there are four hemisphere's in any birthchart, above and below, and east and west of the meridian. Parts of the physical brain.

HEMOGRAPHY—the paranormal act of blood-writing.

HEPATOMANCY—the practice of foreseeing the future. Divination with the use of internal organs of sacrificed animals.

HERB—plants which are natural healers and destroyers. A plant used for food and meditation.

HERBALISM—the use of plants to heal the physical and spiritual bodies. The belief that "life heals life."

HERBALIST—one who has an exquisite knowledge of the use of herbs.

HERBOLOGY—the study and use of Herbs.

HERCULES—the greatest Greek mythological hero possessing great strength who had a strong belief on the gods.

HERESY—a belief deviating from the "true belief" or Orthodox belief of the fifteenth and sixteenth century such as Spirituality or Witchcraft. see holy inquisition.

HERETIC—a sixteenth century person who practiced a belief other than the Orthadox beliefs. see heresy.

HERKIMER DIAMOND—a pseudo-diamond with energy that helps one to begin over again, in this lifetime, when one makes the incorrect choices to fulfill one's soul path.

HERMETICA—the ancient philosophical writings that explore the hidden mysteries of the universe. A combination of the Kabbalah, Christianity and Egyptain beliefs, believed to be the bases of the Western world's occult beliefs.

HERMETIC ORDER OF THE GOLDEN DAWN—a belief which arose in England, believed to be out of Rosicrucianism. Short-lived, apx. 1885.

HERODICUS—a fifth century B.C. physician who applied gymnastics to the treatment of disease.

HEULANDITE—wide range of colored crystals and minerals which help one to regress to the ancient times of Lemura and Atlantis.

HEXAGRAM—the six pointed star created by extending the sides of a hexagram. The star of David. Formed by combining two triangles.

HIERARCHY—the group of spiritual beings on the planes of the solar system who are the forces behind nature and who control the evolutionary process. They themselves are divided into twelve hierarchies. A form of celestial ladder, a group of persons, beings or things arranged in a progressive order according to one's knowledge, superiority or learned qualities. see occult hierarchy.

HIEROGLYPH—sacred symbols of religious or spiritual works. see symbol.

HIGH DICE TEST—a test for PK in which the tested tries to throw two dice so that they will fall with the two uppermost faces totaling eight or more. see low dice test.

HIGHER SELF—the highest consciousness, the crown of the upper spirit in mankind.

HIGH PRIESTESS—a female practitioner of Wicca who has reached a very high status within the religion, passing many tests and usually receiving three initiations.

HINDUISM—a religion indigenous to India, it has no founder, no creed and no centralized hierarchy. The oldest documents are the Vedas, compiled apx. 1000 to 500 B.C.

HIPPOPOTAMUS—symbol of the Egyptain Goddess of Birth.

HISN—a Chinese belief that one is to conduct oneself in a fashion that will uplift the entire human race.

HINDU CHAKRA'S—the Hindu chakra belief has eight rather than seven chakra's. The extra chakra is the Sacral chakra which is located near the root chakra.

HINDUISM—an East Indian view and way of life based on nature and mystical experience.

HISTORIANS—Dagon spirits who telepathically project visions to students of spiritual history for the safety of humankind. see dagon.

HOLDENITE—red colored crystals and minerals which help promote movement in times of plateau delays.

HOLISM—the belief that the determining factor is the whole and not its parts.

HOLISTIC—treatment and knowledge of the whole person. A combination of the physical, mental and spiritual bodies..

HOLISTIC HEALTH—a movement which states that a person must be treated as a whole system with physical, emotional and spiritual parts. That each individual is responsible for his\her own life and for seeking out the means to best maintain a better quality of life.

HOLISTIC SEEING—a "whole-system" form of perception in which a wide range of information is taken in and processed without the distortion of need or goal oriented perception.

HOLOGRAM—a three dimensional image or ghost.

HOLLOW EARTH THEORY—in 1692, Edmund Halley, (Halley's Comet) suggested that the earth was hollow, that there were civilizations living there with their own sun. In 1839-1908, Cyrus Reed Teed suggested that the earth was hollow and that we live on the inside of it.

HOLTITE—orange to green crystals and minerals used in a meditative state to keep one in a comfortable on going path.

HOLY GRAIL—a vessel or person gifted with sacred powers, in both Anglo-Saxon and German Mythology.

HOLY INQUISITION—(1233- 1500)an organization established by the Pope to combat Heresey and Witchcraft. In 1512 the name was changed to Congregation of the Holy Office.

HOLY SPIRIT—a part of the trinity within the Christian belief, father, son and holy spirit.

HOME CIRCLE—another term for seance. see seance.

HOMEOPATHIC HEALING—founded in the early 1800's by Dr. Samuel Hahnemann, the basic belief is that a substance in overdose will show an illness in a healthy person, but will cure the same illness in a sick person if given in infinitesimal doses. A method of treating the whole body with the use of natural ingredients.

HOMEOPATHIC MATERIA MEDICA—a term for the entire list or spectrum of homeopathic medicines such as herbs, gems and crystals.

HOMEOPATHIC MEDICINE—a belief in like cures like. see homeopathic healing.

HOMEOPATHY—the healing method of "like cures like" as in vaccinations.

HOMEOSTASIS—the ability of the body to seek and maintain a normal state of functioning when it's state is threatened by fear, or by the unknown. Spiritual assistance. Spiritual quieting. A stable state of balance between the physical and the spiritual. Maintenance of balance between opposing systems.

HOMING—term applied to persons or animals with the ability to return to their original home when released from a distance. see Psi following.

HONEY—many meanings. India's symbol of the higher self. Greek Orphists symbol of wisdom. Product of the Goddess animal.

HOOD—symbol of hidden motifs. Death with new beginnings.

HOPEITE— wide range of yellow and gray crystals and minerals used to provide comfort within oneself.

HORIZON—an event, person or situation yet to come. Hardly visible. In Astrology, the horizontal axis of a birthchart connecting the ascendant and the descendant.

HORNEBLENDE—wide range of colored crystals and minerals which display pleochroism (different colors at different angles) used to assist in recognizing spiritual dualism.

HOROSCOPE—a chart showing the positions of the planets and the signs of the zodiac relative to a given location on the earth for a given moment. The horoscope is used by astrologers both as a basis for delineating character and for predicting future trends or events.

HORSE—a symbol of physical and universal energy. Controlled subdued life forces. Jung believed the horse to represent the mother within and the intuitive, magical side of humankind.

HORSESHOE—an ancient world symbol signifying entrances and exits. The Greek alphabet, Omega, signifying the end.

HOUR OF MANIFESTATION—an hour of each day set aside to allow the manifestation of spiritual beings or objects. The exact same time each day.

HOURGLASS—symbol of the cycle between physical and spiritual worlds and creation and destruction.

HOUSE—in Astrology this indicates any of the twelve divisions of space above or below the local horizon. The basic arenas or terrains of life that the soul enters and experiences.

HOWLITE—white crystals and minerals used to help calm loud, negative communications.

HUG THERAPY—a belief that hugging is healing.

HUMANITY— the totality of mankind, both male and female.

HUNA—meaning secret, a Polynisian spiritual belief which was inherited from the Ancients.

HUNDREDTH MONKEY—an idea that mass spiritual change can occur once a critical mass of believers has been reached. A belief that if a sufficient number of people meditate, the effects will be felt worldwide.

HUNTER MOON—October 23-November 20. Named hunter moon as this was the month that one hunted for food in preparation for winter.

HUNTING CLAN—members of the Spiritual Great White Brotherhood, who, when called upon, protect all persons from negativity. see Great White Brotherhood.

HYBRIDS—genetic manipulation undertaken by Atlantean scientists to ensure the existence of humankind, prior to the deluge of 8,500 B.C.

HYDRO-THERAPY—a form of healing using water, heat and massage.

HYPERBOREA—a people held by the Ancient Greeks to live beyond the north wind in a region of perpetual sunshine. Highly spiritual. The people of the second root race. see second root race.

HYPERSENTIENCE—the induction method developed by Marcia Moore, a mixture of relaxation and visualization.

HYPERSTHESIA—the state of being sensitive to more than what the average person perceives. A medium or channel.

HYPERMNESIA—the ability to remember more than the average person, of this or past lives.

HYPNAGOGIC—a time when the mind is very receptive to suggestions. The time just before falling asleep, often accompanied by spiritual, dreamlike or past-life images. see hypnopompic.

HYPNOPOMPIC—the drowsy period between being asleep and waking up, often accompanied by dreamlike imagery. see hypnagogic.

HYPNOSIS—a sleep-like state, usually induced by oneself, or others, in which one is receptive to suggestion.

I

I AM RELIGION—founded in 1931 by Guy W. and Edna Ballard. The bases of this religion was the ability to communicate with Jesus and St Germain, and eventually through them, to understand the divinity of the I Am spirit within all humankind.

IAMBLICHUS—(250-325 A.D.) neo-Platonist philosopher who gave formulas for invoking magical powers, one which was plagiarized by Nostradamus. He responded to Porphyry's letter, the response was called "The Reply of Abammon." Iamblichus defended ritualistic magic and divinity. see Anibos.

IANNE AND IAMBRES—the two magicians of the Christian bible who challenged Moses in the Pharaoh's court.

I CHING—another name for Yi King, the Chinese book of changes which contains methods and explanations of prophecy.

IDEALISM—the concept that ideas or thoughts are real. The theory that ideas or thoughts are the cause of reality.

IDENTITY—finding ones place in the spiritual networking of the physical existence and recognizing that one is more than the physical body. Personal worth. Life goals. see identification.

IDENTITY DELUSION—the illusion that our true identity is that of the physical body. Disregarding the spiritual body. see identification.

IDENTIFICATION—a mental state when one realizes that one is not the physical body but the spiritual body. see identity.

IDEOCRASE—wide range of colored crystals and minerals used to promote loyalty to humankind.

IDEOLOGY— the study of ideas. Metaphysical study of thoughts and creation.

IDEOMOTION—the physical movement which is made in response to an idea, thought or image which originates in the subconscious mind, as in visualization or creative ritual. The response when the target is found in Dowsing.

IDEOMOTOR EFFECT—the psychological phenomenon that is the cause of all psychic response. When a dowser receives psychic energy it creates a slight muscle movement which makes the involved device re-act.

IDEOMOTOR RESPONSES—unconscious subtle responses to a question or thought, felt and understood by mediums and psychics, to let them know if they are remaining "on track" when giving a reading.

IDEOMOTOR—a physical involuntary response triggered by an intuitive thought or suggestion. Spiritual thoughts triggering physical movements.

IDEOPLASM—similar to ectoplasm with the additional advantage that this substance may be molded. see ectoplasm.

INGRESS—the act of entering into different planes.

IHVH—the ancient Hebrew belief that these were the initials of Jehovah.

ILLUMINATI—a 15th century term used for those who had the knowledge to communicate with spirits or the Deity. Associated with cults and secret orders such as the Freemasons, Rosicrucians and other mystery organizations which help humanity.

ILLUMINATION—growth, expansion and enlightenment of the mind and inner being. Spiritually enlightened.

ILLUSION—the state or fact of being spiritually mislead. Spiritual fraud.

IMAGERY—the mental reproduction of a remembered or imagined visual experience.

IMAGINATION—viewing an object prior to it entering the physical reality, one of the greatest faculties of the mind. The visualization faculty of the mind. The creative faculty of the mind.

IMAGING—the power of the mind to reproduce mental images, revisualization of the physical reality.

IMMORTAL—something or someone who has everlasting existence.

IMMORTALITY—the state of everlasting life.

I.M.S—International Meditation Society, a group brought together to teach and learn certain forms of meditation.

IMP—a juvenile demon or a child of evil.

IMPLANTS—believed by the Ancients to be words or events imprinted in one's memory banks centuries ago by those wishing to control one.

IMPRESSION—a spiritual act or event which produces an effect on the intellect or feelings.

INANIMATE—an object or thing without apparent life.

INCAS—a wide spread peoples of the Americas, apx. 600 B.C. The high cultures of Mexico and Peru had a strong spiritual belief, good people crossed a bridge made of hair to a peaceful silent land and the bad people went to a frigid place.

INCANTATION—repitition of chants used in rituals.

INCARNATION—spiritual entity taking on a physical

body. See reincarnation.

INCENSE—scented sticks or stones which burn very slowly and give of aromas. Used in ritual or meditation.

INCUBUS—mythological male demon choosing to have sexual intercourse with human women. see Succubus.

INCORPOREAL PERSONAL AGENCY—(IPA) a synonym for after death experience.

INDAGATOR—one who is in search of knowledge, especially spiritual growth and knowledge.

INDIGENOUS PEOPLE—original people of original lands who have learned to live naturally with their God and nature.

INDIVIDUALISING PRINCIPLE—the existence of the mind. That which distinguishes thinking man from the animals. The third level of spiritual growth, i.e. plant, animal then human. see mana principle.

INDIVIDUALITY—a separate, absolute distinctiveness, the imperishable ego in which the personality embraces the memory of but one life.

INDIVIDUAL SUBJECTIVITY—the inner god, soul, or spiritual part of each person which has its own "fingerprint".

INDIVIDUATION—a term used by Jung meaning coming to self-hood or self-realization.

INDUCED PSI PHENOMENON—a spiritual or paranormal event caused intentionally for the purpose of helping one. Sending one healing spiritual energies.

INDUCTOR—an object held by a sensitive that is giving information about the objects owner. One who induces a trance.

INDUCTION—putting one into a relaxed state or trance. A form of hypnotism.

INERTIA—a state of opposing change. Fear of the unknown. Being stuck in one place. A lack of spiritual knowledge. Spiritual complacency.

INFINITY SIGN—an eight lying on its side having one circle moving clockwise and the other anti-clockwise. The coming together of male and female. The true balance of positive and negative. Continuation. Without end.

INFINITE—something which is endless. Continuing on forever.

INITIATES—the wise ones who have acquired the secret knowledge of the spiritual mysteries. The science of the self and the one self which is all selves.

INITIATION—a ritual or ceremony by which one is introduced to a particular event, group or knowledge.

INIATIONS—the first event of any science. The pathway of Initiation is the final stage of the pathway of evolution taken by humankind. This path is divided into five levels, called the Five Initiations. see initiates.

INNER EGO—that which brings one to delicate inner perceptions, without which physical existence could not be maintained.

INNER HEALING—healing of the mind and spirit, usually done by oneself.

INNER SELF—the soul or spirit within the physical body. The God-like intuitive directions received without request.

INNER TEMPLE—the home or existing place of the soul or spirit within the physical body. Often referred to in the Christian Bible.

INNER VOICE—the inner mental phenomenon of an

auditive sensation covered subjectively or objectively by the term clairaudience. Hearing a mental voice without anyone speaking. A method of spiritual communication.

INSIGHT—a newly acquired perspective on what "is". A new way of looking at physical and spiritual realities. Spiritual intervention.

INSIGHT MEDITATION—a Buddhist practice of attention training where awareness of bodily activities and mind content are used to develop concentration.

INSPIRATION—a psychic state where one becomes susceptible to creative spiritual influence, such as instant awareness and thoughts automatically entering one's mind.

INSPIRATIONAL SPEAKERS—speakers who deliver strong messages which transform or inspire their audience. Powerful spiritual speakers. see inspiration.

INSTITUTE FOR NOETIC SCIENCES—astronaut Edgar D. Mitchell founded this institution after he retired from the space program. It is the result of his space experiences and devotion to parapsychology.

INTELLECTUAL KNOWING—another term for a gut feeling or intuition. Thought to be knowledge learned by conventional learning methods.

INTELLIGENCE—one who has learned that which one is wanting to understand in either the spiritual or physical realm.

INTERACTIONISM—the dualistic belief that mind and matter greatly affect one another and cannot exist independently on this physical plane.

INTERNATIONAL MEDITATION SOCIETY—a group brought together by Maharishi Mahesh Yogi to teach specific forms of meditation.

INTEREST—intense and focused awareness in the physical and spiritual realms.

INTERPRETATION—finding the meaning for something which would be otherwise meaningless. Understanding visions, premonitions, etc.

INTERRUPTERS—that which stops or interrupts an action, thought, idea and\or meditation, generally one's own thoughts or psychic visions.

INTRASPECT—in Astrology, an aspect made by a planet or point in one's birthchart to a planet or point in another's birthchart.

INTROSPECTION—looking inwards for that which ones seeks. Seeking spiritual peace.

INTROVERSION—a reserved inward attitude of mind. Unsociable both mentally and spiritually.

INTUITION—knowledge which flashes into the conscious mind from sources other than the conscious self. God or deity knowledge.

INTUITIVE KNOWING—any knowledge acquired through the process of intuition. A sudden knowing. see intuition.

INVOLUTION—a progressive inhabitation of the body by the soul.

IPALNEMOANI—an Aztec concept of the supreme Deity often spoken of as "he who gives us life." First used in classic Aztec prayers, still used today.

IRIDOLOGY—a means of revealing the pathological and functional problems of the body by reading the markings in the iris and surrounding area's of the eye.

IRIS—the flower and name represent the Greek Goddess of the rainbow.

IRON—gray to black mineral which promotes mental and spiritual stability.

ISLAM—a term for the religion of the Muslim world.

ISLAND—symbol of a spiritual place of the mind or subconscious.

IVORY—fossilized ivory assists a spiritual worker to maintain long, lasting energies.

JADE—green colored crystals and minerals used to help one receive answers to problem situations through dreams.

JANISM—an Eastern Spiritual Belief which was an outgrowth of Hinduism, founded in the sixth century B.C.

JANUARY MOON—known as Wild Animal Moon by many cultures. A month when many wild animals cannot find food in their natural domains. They must come down mountains and into the open where they make contact with humans which could be dangerous. see Wild Animal Moon.

JASPER—wide range of colors but most common is red. The crystals and minerals are used to assist in removing scars from one's life.

JEHOVAH—the ancient Hebrew Deity. A personal God.

JESTER—symbol of the unpredictable qualities of the Goddess Fata.

JESUS—the Christian medium to the God Jehovah. Believed to be the son of God. (the equivalent of Buddha to Buddhists, Mohammed to Muslems etc.)

JET—a fossilized wood used to help in the removal of fearful thoughts and visions.

JOAN OF ARC—1412-1431—one of the first known maidens to experience voices and visions from spirits and her spirit guides. She was burned at the stake but history has it that her heart remained untouched, it was found whole among the ashes.

JIVA—a separated unit of consciousness.

JOVIALIZATION—in Astrology, an introspect made by one's Jupiter to any point in another's birthchart, symbolizing the uplifting and expansion or the flattening and over-extension of the affected point.

JUDGEMENT OF THE DEAD—many beliefs. The ritual of a culture which must happen when one dies. The Zoroastrian believe that when one dies one must cross a bridge, and, if one was good the crossing will be easy but if one was bad the crossing will be difficult. The modern day Christian belief is that one first goes to purgatory before entering heaven.

JULIA'S BUREAU—a free public institute founded in London by W.Stead in 1909 for the purpose of communicating with spirits of the dead where three different mediums were visited to ensure real and true communications.

JULY MOON—known as Thunder Moon due to the many thunder storms at this time of year. The Ancients believed this to be the voice of the Deity. see Thunder Moon.

JUNE MOON—named Strawberry Moon after the beauty of the flower of the strawberry and the abundance of it's fruit. see strawberry moon.

JUNG, CARL GUSTAV—1875-1961—worked with Freud. Well known for his paranormal research on dreams and symbolism. He was known as an "in-tune with the spirits" person.

JUSTICE—a principle of virtue requiring one to have respect and fairness in the treatment of others. A learned spiritual trait.

K

KA—ancient Egyptian word meaning soul or double, pictured on tombs as a human faced bird. Believed to be the purpose of mummification, in that the Ka or soul could live longer. Many psychics use this on their amulets.

KABBALAH—(Kabala, Cabala) ancient Hebrew word meaning "doctrines". A Hebrew book on God teaching ontology, cosmology, theology and anthropology.

KACHINAS—the supernatural beings or spirits of the ancestral dead. The belief of the Hopi Indians as well as the Pueblo Tribes.

KAHUNA—according to the Polynesian belief system these spiritual individuals were the keepers of the ancient secrets of the universe which pertains to the knowledge that enables one to heal and perform other helpful feats.

KALI YUGA—an age or cycle. According to Eastern philosophy our evolution is divided into four cycles with the present age being Kali-Yuga, meaning the "Black Age" which spans 430,000 years.

KARMA—a Hindu term for the law of justice. The law of cause and effect. As you sow so shall you reap. That which rules one's life and the conditions of the next reincarnation.

KARMA YOGA—the practice of work and selfless service.

KARREZZA—the Titanic discipline where ritualized erotic procedures are entered, but terminated just before orgasm. The theory is that the preserved energy is then sent into spiritual knowledge.

KEEPER—a metal bar kept across the open end of a horseshoe magnet to retain its magnet charge, magnets used in healing and ritual.

KEY—a symbol of the Egyptian Tarot which signifies free access to highly developed doctrine. Allowed entry. see keys crossed.

KEY CRYSTAL—a crystal with a hexagon indented into itself.

KEYS CROSSED—a symbol of the Egyptian Tarot signifying the forbidden entrance or forbidden doctrine. Entry denied. see key.

KILNER SCREEN—a double sheet of glass containing a solution of diocese, used for viewing one's aura.

KINESIOLOGY—a form of nutritional diagnosis and monitor of treatment using measured muscle tone. A natural approach to physical and spiritual growth.

KING\LORD—the divine spirit which controls a plane. Symbol of the ruler of the conscious and subconscious mind. see Raja Lord.

KINGDOM OF GOD—the quiet place within. Serenity. At peace with oneself. Spiritual unity with the Deity.

KIRLIAN PHOTOGRAPHY—photographing the Aura and other energies invisible to the eye. Devised in the 1950's by the Russian, Semyou Kirlian.

KISMET—an Arabic term meaning fate.

KNOTS—essential to magical ritual. The knot design is common on amulets or talismen. Symbol of a blockage of energy.

KNIGHT JZ—(1946-) channel for Ramtha the enlightened one.

KOAN—a question in Zen-Buddhism which has no logical answer.

KORAN— the sacred book of the Muslem belief system, written in Arabic.

KORESHAN UNITY—a semi-religious sect founded by Teed, believing that the earth was hollow. It is believed that David Koresh at Waco Texas had followed this belief. see hollow earth.

KOROHAHA TU—the New Zealand Maori Tribe name of the Deity which lives in a Dowser's dowsing object.

KUMARAS—according to Hindu Belief these are the seven self conscious beings in the universe called "the spiritual-mind born sons of Brahma."

KUNDALINI—an energy that can be controlled by those with spiritual knowledge of this energy. The energy point is located between the excretion and reproductive organs and up along the spine. Also called the serpent force.

KUNDALINI YOGA—a ritual which releases the coiled serpent energy which resides at the base of the physical spine.

KNOWLEDGE—that which is learned through intelligence and experience.

KYANITE—crystals and minerals with a wide range of colors which assist in spiritual positively.

L

LADDER PATH—spiritual mysteries founded 60,000 years ago by the Atlanteans and continued at Shamballla. see Shamballa.

LADY WONDER—the first horse in Richmond Virginia that was believed to have ESP. The horse could answer questions by pushing over children's toy alphabet blocks.

LAMA—Tibetan Priest or Monk

LAMPROPHYLLITE—yellow to deep brown crystals and minerals which stimulate mental powers.

LANGUAGE—the partial and daily method of communication by most people.

LAPIS LAZULI—grammatical end product of the physical time sequence. The present deep blue crystals which act as a link between the physical, spiritual and celestial worlds.

LASER WAND CRYSTAL—a long slender crystal with small sides creating the apex.

LAW OF ABUNDANCE—the belief that when one gives, one will receive in abundance; if one takes one will be taken from in abundance.

LAW OF CAUSE AND EFFECT—another term for Karma. see karma.

LAW OF LIGHT-LIFE ENERGY—the energy which supports and maintains all living and non-living things. The Deity. The law of the universe. The networking of existence.

LAW OF NATURE—a general relation of all living things which determines how nature works and evolution progresses.

LAW OF POLARITY—a Metaphysical belief that only the joining of the two polarities, positive and negative, will create a new manifestation. i .e. man and woman create child.

LAW OF PROBABILITY—the possible outcome of a given problem or thought according to probability.

LAW OF SPIRITUAL ECONOMY—that which oversees hierarchical effort, avoids duplication and ensures that energy is not wasted or goes unused.

LAW OF TRANSMUTATION—that which governs the conversion of harmful effects into beneficial results.

LAYA YOGA—a meditation on one or more of the chakra's.

LAYING ON OF HANDS—a form of faith or altered healing which does not depend on traditional medicine. A healer touches and sends Universal energy to the afflicted area.

LAZARIS—a channelled entity who first spoke through Jach Pursel in 1974. Several books have been written as a result of this channelling.

LEAD—lead gray mineral used to assist in communications with one's spiritual guides.

LEAVES—a symbol of growth, vitality or energy yet to be manifested.

LEFT HANDED PATH—another term for negativity or evil. see right-handed path.

LEFT-SIDED CRYSTAL—a six sided quartz crystal with the tip angled towards the left is a receiving crystal, sometimes with a small flat area on one edge. see right-sided crystal. see receiving crystal.

LEMNISCATE—a powerful occult symbol which looks like the figure 8 laying on its side, signifying eternity, infinity, higher consciousness and the Holy Spirit. Appears often in the Tarot.

LEMEGETON—key of Solomon. A grimoire from the seventeenth century believed to be full of hierarchical lists. see grimoire.

LEMURIA—legendary lost continent which existed 18 million years ago. It existed prior to Atlantis. Thought to be the original garden of Eden. A peaceful people highly advanced in psychic phenomenon.

LEO—the Zodiac sign "the lion" July23-August 22.

LESSONS—experiences. That for which the soul or spirit enters the physical body.

LEUCITE— white-gray crystals which provide windows through which new spirits may enter.

LEVITATION—reversing gravity. The ability of human beings to rise, unsupported into the air. The knowledge of moving oneself, or objects, with the mind through mental control of oneself or the object's vibrations.

LEY LINES—lines of energy running through the earth in a specific pattern connecting monuments and natural features. Somewhat similar to those which, in human beings, are intercepted in acupuncture. Known in China as dragon lines.

LIBETHENITE—wide range of green colored crystals used to promote freedom from self-imposed restrictions.

LIBRA—the Zodiac sign "the scales" September 23-October 22.

LIFE AFTER DEATH— a belief on reincarnation and spiritual growth, that one's spirit or soul continues to return to this physical reality or other realities. An assessment period is taken in between re-incarnations.

LIFE-FORCE—many meanings. That which keeps one alive. Vital energy. Mana. Bio-cosmic energy.

LIFE GOAL—the life goal for the coming or just-ended life is found when one regresses to the incarnation preparation, or progresses to post mortem experiences. There are often several goals. The most popular goal being growth in understanding, sympathy, proficiency and independence.

LIFE PLAN—the goals of ones coming life. Important encounters, karma or talents to be developed.

LIFE READING—entering the Akashic records and reading the events that have happened in lives past, present and future.

LIFE RETROSPECT—after one's death, a quick overview of one's complete past life, questioning if one had completed one's life plan and what is necessary to re-incarnate. see life plan.

LIFE SYMBOLIZATION—a part of the self-examination, in pure soul state prior to re-incarnation, in which one forms one's next life and then proceeds to experience it.

LIFE READING—a psychic reading in which the psychic looks back into one's past lives stating who one was and what one did, thus providing information and answers to present situations and problems.

LIGHT—many meanings. Gaining new spiritual knowledge. Protective white energy light. Protective activity of God. Fastest vibration of the ether.

LIGHTENING—symbol of an instant gain of new knowledge. Understanding. A fast new arrival.

LILY—the Christian belief that this was the flower the Virgin Mary smelled and became pregnant. Symbol of fertility.

LILLITH—an ancient Mythological Queen of the Demons.

LIMB MOLD—(or cast) an ancient tree limb fossil, filled with a mineral which represents the theory of reincarnation.

LIMBO—a place or realm for the souls of ones passed on who are "stuck" for a short period of time. see discarnate.

LION—ancient belief that the lion was the symbol of strength, power and majesty. King of the beasts with subhuman powers. Associated with the Nature Goddess Cybele.

LIVE ARCHEOLOGY—the study of psychic energies associated with ancient sites as opposed to the classification of artifacts.

LLORONA—the weeping woman of Aztec folklore. Most often equated with Acihuat, the water woman, who lurks around wells and streams seeking to catch men unfaithful to their wives. see Acihuat.

LOCHNESS MONSTER— a creature of great size thought to inhabit Lochness, Scotland. It's existence has never been proven.

LODGE—a building or place of learning, rest and retreat. A brotherhood. One belonging to a specific group or belief.

LOGOS—the Deity or God as manifested by every nation and people. The outward or physical expression of an inner thought, therefore speech is the logos of thought. God. A symbol or sign which signifies a specific person, entity or place.

LOMILOMI—a Hawaiian word for a healing through the use of massage and salt water.

LOMONOSOVITE—red to violet colored crystals used to increase the development of one's psychic center.

LORD OF CIVILIZATION—the spiritual protector of all the cultural streams of evolution, with awareness of all civilizations past, present and future.

LORDS OF SHAMBALLA—wise ones who came to Shamballa to guide humankind to enlightenment. see shamballa.

LORD OF THE FLAME- an advanced spiritual group or hierarchy who guide the universe, who took control of human development apx. 18 million years ago during the existence of Lemuria.

LOST WORD—a word once uttered continues on unto eternity and cannot be retrieved. Words which continue to vibrate and exist.

LOTUS—a water flower of many petals, symbolizing knowledge, purity and beauty. Sacred in China, Egypt and India. Symbol of the Universal Goddess.

LOTUS SEAT—a sitting position used in yoga, aligning the spine so spiritual energy may flow freely.

LOURDES—a famous Roman Catholic Shrine in Southern France where thousands of healings have been documented. Attributed to the Virgin Mary appearing in 1858 in a grotto to assist Bernadette Soubirous.

LOVE—a state of interest and acceptance. Wanting to please and enjoy another person and to be sexually compatible. Unconditional acceptance. That which gives and receives.

LOW DICE TEST—a test in PK in which the tested

tries to throw two dice with the uppermost faces totalling six or less. see high dice test.

LUCID DREAMING—the art of one knowing that one is dreaming, believed to be beneficial in spiritual growth.

LUCIDITY—a faculty by which supernatural knowledge may be obtained. A collective term for the phenomenon of clairvoyance, clairaudience and psychometry.

LUCIFER—a Christian word meaning Satan, the devil or evil spirits.

LUNARIZATION—in Astrology, an introspect by one's moon to any point of another's chart, symbolizing the process of sensitizing and inspiring, or emotionally upsetting the affected point.

LUMINOUS PHENOMENON—flashing supernatural lights usually seen around grave yards or churches. see spectral flames.

LYCANTHROPY—a condition whereby one believes one is turning into a wolf.

M

MAAT— an Egyptian word for "truth" whose symbol is a feather.

MACROBIOTICS—a way of life based on a diet of brown rice, grains, vegetables and little else, believed to promote spiritual awareness.

MACROCOSM—the manifestation of the cosmos or universe by the Deity. see microcosm.

MACUMBA—a Brazilian form of Voodoo. The worship of African Dieties through magic and possession of the spirit. Spiritualism in Brazil.

MAFU—an entity channelled through Penny Torres in 1984, believed to be similar to Ramtha. see Ramtha.

MAGATAMA—the Japanese word for one of the curved "tadpole" symbols of life. Two of these Magatama form a circle.

MAGER ROSETTE—a color disc used in Dowsing, originally designed to determine the drinkability of a water source.

MAGI—initiates who oversee transmutations. see the law of transmutation.

MAGIC—spiritual-the projection or movement of subtle but natural energies to bring about necessary change. Assuming there are powers in nature and the universe to be used by one who has it's knowledge. non-spiritual-that which creates an illusion, slight of hand.

MAGIC WAND— a specialized talisman used to facilitate the invocation of magical spells. Made of hazel or ash wood.

MAGICIAN—spiritual. One who practices (negative) black or (positive)white magic. see magic.

MAGIC CIRCLE—a ring drawn for specific rituals by

magicians, mediums and readers to protect themselves from unwanted spirits which they may invoke.

MAGNETIC ENERGY BALANCING—a healer, with the knowledge of magnets, faces a person, raises the hands with palms facing the other person, touches palms and begins a magnetic energy transfer through the palm chakras.

MAGNETIC FLUID—an ancient term for energy meridians. see meridians.

MAGNETIC HEALING or POLARITY HEALING—a balancing of one's magnetic polarities with the use of magnets. see magnetic polarities.

MAGNETIC HILLS—a sensory illusion created by an underground magnetic pull which makes an object appear that it has a slight upward tilt when it is actually tilted downward. Psychics are sensitive to these pulls and are able to realign their magnetic bodies when around these areas.

MAGNETIC LEVITATION—overcoming gravity by using the repulsion between two like magnetic poles. It is believed this is how most psychics levitate.

MAGNETIC PHENOMENON—a medium with the power to activate magnetic devices. One who is able to create magnets with one's mental abilities.

MAGNETISM—many meanings. The science of magnetic fields and their effects causing the unbalanced spin of electrons in atoms. The aura of a person. The aura energy which makes one feel comfortable around others. Energy which draws two people closer together. An unknown pull towards another person or object. see aura.

MAGNETIC POLI AMBO—a magnet with both ends potentized, used to inspect the human aura and find energy flow problems. Also used by homeopathic doctors in the treatment of various health problems. This form of magnet is connected to the neutral elements and forces of air and ether. see potentized

MAGNETIS POLUS ARCTICUS—a magnet with the north pole potentized used in finding energy flow problems of the aura. The north pole has a subduing effect on living organisms. see magnetis polus australis. see potentized.

MAGNETIS POLUS AUSTRALIS—a magnet with the south pole potentized, used in finding energy flow problems of the aura. The south pole magnet has an energizing effect on living organisms. see magnetis polus arcticus, neutral magnet, potentized.

MAGNETITE—black colored mineral useful in building self-esteem and building new friendships.

MAGNETOMETER—an instrument used to measure the magnetic force fields of all things, including humans and their aura's.

MAGNETRON—a radionic instrument having an arrangement of magnets on it to witness the Sun's magnet field and its effect on the earth and persons sensitive to magnetism.

MAGUS—originally a Zoarstrian priest. Modern day meaning is a seer, diviner, magician or philosopher. He was a member of a mystic band 4000 B.C. Believed to have provided occult teachings to Staintain Moses. The XIX book of Mose's scripts discuss the topaz ring he received from

Magus to help him see clearer visions.

MAHOE STICKS—a belief of the New Zealand Maori that these wooden sticks are inhabited with divine spirits.

MAIDEN—the first aspect of the Great Goddess.

MAITREYA—a figure in the Buddhist belief who is viewed as the coming enlightened one.

MALACHITE—green colored minerals and crystals. Useful in assisting one changing physical and spiritual positions..

MALEFICIA—crimes assigned to the witch and witchcraft in the sixteenth century.

MALIFIZ COMMISION—a sixteenth century ruling Monarch's commission of lawyers who carried out the Holy Inquisition's judicial responsibilities and passed sentence. see Holy Inquisition.

MALLEUS MALEFICARUM—(Hammer of Witches) a book published in the late 1400's by two Dominican Monks on the art of Witch Hunting. It served as a guide to the Holy Inquisition for more than a century. see holy inquisition.

MANA—many meanings. Polynesian word for complete control and power. Huna term for the basic vital force of thought forms. The mind or mental faculty.

MANA PRINCIPLE—that which separates or distinguishes man from animal. Most often called the individualising principle.

MANAS—Sanskrit term for mind or mentality. The creator and the created.

MANDALA—a symbolic diagram viewed as mystical maps of the cosmos or Dieties. Usually round but may be triangular or oval.

MANDORLA—an Ancient's term meaning almond. The female genital symbol.

MANDRAKE ROOT—a plant related to the potato which grows in the shape of the human body. Used in magical spells and ritual. In ancient Mythology it is said that when the root is pulled out, it emits a human like shriek that will drive a human insane. Dogs are immune to this sound so they were used to pull the root.

MANICHAEISM—founded in 200 A.D. by a Persian priest, Mani. His doctrine was to teach a severe dualism between spirit and matter, and the only way to reach an everlasting spiritual life was to believe on him and his teachings.

MANIFESTATION—the unexplainable appearance of objects or ghostlike images. Spirit appearances during a seance. The creation of one's own physical reality.

MANIFESTATION CRYSTAL—a large crystal with a smaller crystal totally enclosed within itself.

MANTRA—verse from the Vedas. A word without meaning used as a focal point during meditation. A sacred word given to one by a spiritual mentor to use during meditation.

MAP DOWSING—a form of dowsing in which the dowsing instrument, or palm of the hand, indicates the location of the required mineral on a map rather than the geographical area.

MARBLE—mineral with a wide range of colors used to enhance the remembering of dreams.

MARCH MOON—known as Thaw Moon. Given this name by many cultures as this is the month the sun warms the Earth and causes new movement in the plant and animal kingdoms. see Thaw Moon.

MARIAN APPARITIONS—reported visions of the virgin Mary. Ghost like images of Mary.

MARRIAGE—symbol of joining positive and negative energies as in man/woman, day/night, conscious/subconscious.

MARTIAL ARTS—a form of self defence having a strong spiritual influence.

MANTIC ART—see divination.

MASKS—face coverings worn during ceremonies or rituals. The purpose of masks is to transform the wearer and viewer, by association, into something other than that which they are.

MASSAGE—the art of treating body ailments by the manipulation of muscles and soft body tissue, thus clearing the body meridians and allowing energy to flow freely.

MASS HALLUCINATION—that which is considered normal in the physical experience. i.e. everyone believes that night comes after day-so it does, everyone believes that women have menopause-so they do.

MASTER—one who has attained perfection in the evolution of the soul. Godlike.

MASTER-APPRENTICE SYSTEM—a teaching procedure where a master works with one person and teaches that person all that one knows, then expects that person to continue on in the same fashion.

MASTER WITHIN—the inner self. The inner spiritual entity.

MATERIALISM—the theory that matter and its movement create the universe, and that all phenomenon, including those of spirit, are due to material movement and existence.

MATERIALIZATION—the knowledge or ability to make the invisible become visible. Causing objects to become visible. In Astrology, an introspect made by one's mars to any point on another's chart, materialization, emboldens, arouses enrages or frightens the affected point. see manifestation.

MATTER—that which is essential to expression on this physical plane. Solid elements.

MAUVE OR PURPLE LIGHT—(energy) color of the third eye chakra. Outside or seventh color of the rainbow. One of the colors used to move an object towards oneself in telekinesis. Color used to heal the head area.

MAY MOON—known as Flower Moon because of the abundance of many beautiful flowers at this time of the year. see Flower Moon.

MECHANICS—the science of energies or forces and their actions on the physical body and the motions they produce.

MEDICAL DIAGNOSIS—checking one's aura or energy flow lines through psychic means, and then arriving at the physical problem and it's possible healing methods. Energy, rather than tissue is checked.

MEDICINE BAG—generally made of leather in which one, especially Natives, keep an assortment of objects believed to have healing powers. see power bag.

MEDICINE WHEEL—large circles of rocks laid out in spiritual energy areas by North American Indian Tribes. The modern day use of these wheels has been an avenue of spiritual growth, protection and healing power.

MEDITATION—a practice of quieting one's emotions and thoughts. Opening the mind to the inner being of the spiritual self. Turning inward toward the self. A transformation of consciousness.

MEDIUM—one who has been given the gift or knowledge of communication with those passed over or dead.

MEDIUM, MENTAL—one who regularly receives communications from the spirits of the dead and communicates them to the living.

MEDIUM, PHYSICAL—a person sitting with a group of other people who produce physical effects believed to be from the spirits of the dead, such as ghosts or ectoplasm.

MEGALITHS—groups of large stone structures or standing stones dated back to the Neolithic or Bronze age. Believed to have supernatural energies, healing powers and magical powers.

MELIPHANE—yellow colored crystals which helps in the softening of one's harsh characteristics.

MEMORY—the function of the mind which perceives, conserves, and reproduces impression and events of this physical reality.

MEMORY BANKS—the conditioning with which one is born. Memory of all life times. Memory of the path chosen in soul state.

MENEHUNES—entities from the Hawaiian Islands. Similar to the Trolls of Noris legend or the Leprechauns of Ireland. Believed to be mischievous but will do good for those whom they like.

MENSENDIECK HEALING SYSTEM—brought to North America in 1905. A new found method of healing the physical and spiritual bodies through the application of correct posture.

MENTAL BODY—the subtle energy body associated with the intellect, containing thought-forms.

MENTAL DISCIPLINE—the art of a psychic controlling one's own mind, and keeping it clear of stray thoughts. The capability of pure concentration.

MENTAL ETIQUETTE—having the ability to enter another's mind and doing so in a very private, honourable manner.

MENTAL HEALING—a healing in which the healer visualizes a person and the inflicted area, then visualizes that area healed. Several different methods may be used in one healing see absent healing.

MENTAL MODEL—the image in one's mind when thinking of an object before it's physical manifestation.

MENTALIST—a person who specializes in magic and makes it appear to be psychic.

MENTAL MANNERS—same as mental etiquette. The one who's mind is entered permits,has knowledge and accepts this action.

MENTAL PATTERNS—the images created by one's conscious mind which creates our physical reality in this and all incarnations.

MENTAL SIGNPOSTS—a travelling entity who encounters points that should be marked for other mental travellers. Alerts or signs left by previous astral or mental travellers marking any points of interest or points of negativity.

MENTOR—one who teaches. Spiritual teacher. Wise one.

MERCHANT'S STONE—see cinnebar.

MERCURIALIZATION—in Astrology, an introspect formed by the Mercury of one to any point on another's chart, symbolizing the intellectual stimulation or confusion of the affected point.

MERIDIAN—in Astrology, the vertical axis of the birthchart, the line connecting the mid-heaven and the nadir.

MERIDIANS—apx. fourteen invisible lines or channels of the body on which energy (chi) flows. see magnetic fluid. see chi.

MERLIN—legendary wizard of the twelfth century who is said to have managed the birth of King Arthur. Modern day interpretation of a Celtic Mystic or Shaman. A Great Magician and controller of spiritual energy.

MESMERISM—now called hypnotism. Having the control of another's body or mind. The most famous practitioner was Dr. Anton Mesmer. First known form of healing with magnets.

MEST—a combination of matter, energy, space and time. The physical universe.

MESSAGE—a communication through speech. Visual or spiritual phenomenon.

MESSELITE—crystals with a wide range of colors used to enhance automatic writing.

METAGNOME—French word for a sensitive or psychic.

METAGNOMY—a scientific term for knowledge that is obtained from a source other than the five senses. The study of parapsychology.

METAGRAPHOLOGY—one who is able to give a complete psychic reading by touching script or by looking at one's handwriting.

METAL BENDING—a psychokinetic phenomena whereby metal, even heavy objects, appear to bend without the exertion of physical force. These tests use only mental concentration.

METAPHYSICAL—one who believes in metaphysics.

METAPHYSICS— a science of ultimate causes of the supernatural. A belief on ultimate and fundamental reality and the nature of things. A belief on reincarnation. A belief that the soul, or spirit, and the physical body are one yet separate. A belief that one's true identity is "spirit having a physical experience". Greek word meta meaning after, physics meaning natural bodies.

METEMPSYCHOSIS—the progressional experiences of the soul from one existence to another, i.e. the stone becomes a plant, the plant becomes an animal, the animal becomes a man, the man becomes a spirit, the spirit becomes a god.

METEORITE—formed in outer space. Psychics believe this mineral to be of great assistance in all psychic phenomenon.

METHETHERIAL—beyond the ether. The realm or world in which the spirits exist.

MICA—layers of crystal which psychics use as spiritual mirrors for themselves or those with whom they are working.

MICROCOSM—the manifestation of the physical reality through the thoughts of physical persons. see macrocosm.

MICRO/MACROCOSM—a belief that all things are equal except for size, mass, function or particulars, all are subject to the same universal laws.

MICTIANI—an Aztec term for "the ones who bring death." They are considered, by the villagers, to be eaters of human flesh. The modern day version is referred to as the grim reaper.

MIDDENS—Ancient dumps next or close to old churches and spiritual gatherings where sensitive persons find objects or receive messages from the past.

MIDDLE WAY—American Indian term meaning moderation in all things. Peace and calm.

MID-HEAVEN—in Astrology, the highest zodiacal point above the horizon, the approximate position of the sun at high noon, the cusp of the tenth house, the tenth house as a whole.

MIND—the consciousness, the intellect, understanding, memory and purpose of a persons physical existence. The subjective emergent of the physical brain functioning in which awareness is created by informational patterns of the spirit.

MIND-BLEND—the spiritual blending or coming together of two minds to create a close relationship, as in marriage.

MIND CURE—healing one's mind that has been affected by negative programming. Releasing bad omens or curses from one's mind or belief.

MIND DYNAMICS—the interactions of the different levels and forces of one's mind, the conscious, sub conscious and the super conscious.

MIND ESSENCE—pure awareness. Spiritual awareness.

MIND-OVER-MATTER—the belief that the subconscious mind creates that which it understands to be true, or that which the conscious mind desires.

MIND/SPIRIT—The mind/spirit term refers to the active reality within. That which creates thoughts and then manifests the thoughts into the physical reality.

MINOR ASPECTS—in Astrology, aspects other than the conjunction, sextile, square, trine or opposition.

MINUTE OF AN ARC—in Astrology, one sixteenth of a degree, often called a minute.

MIRACLE—an incident that has no physical explanation. Generally a good incident.

MIRROR—the Ancients believed the mirror was the keeper of the soul. Many persons were buried with their mirrors because of this belief. A Goddess symbol connected with the Moon.

MIRROR OF VENUS—a solar cross with four equal sides surrounded by a circle indicating fertility.

MISTLETOE—long associated with Christian Christmas holidays. Also associated with romance such as kissing or hugging under the mistletoe. Used in many spiritual rituals.

MITOGENETIC RADIATION—an early term for Aura, coined by the Russian Scientist Alexander Gurvich.

MODE—in Astrology, one of the three expressions of sign energy: cardinal, fixed and mutable.

MOLDAVITE—green colored crystals and minerals of extraterrestrial origin placed here to serve the inhabitants of the planet.

MOMENT POINT—spiritual entity word meaning all events happen at the same momemt

MONAD—a Greek word meaning "one". The Threefold existence on its own plane, (father, son and holy spirit: will, intuition and higher mind.) The immortal part of man. A unit of one life, either physical or spiritual. "All that is" of the universe.

MONITION—supernatural warning such as hearing a

voice say "go home" and upon going home find an emergency.

MONITIONS OF APPROACH—unaccountable forewarning of meeting someone. i.e. a person is seen in the street and thought to be an old friend, the mistake is recognized, yet that person comes into view a moment or two later.

MONOTHEISM—the belief or concept of a single deity. A belief on one Universal God.

MONTGOMERY, RUTH—an author who communicates with spiritual beings or guides with the use of automatic writing.

MOON—a symbol of the subconscious mind. A feminine sign of personality. A symbol of many Goddesses.

MOONS—many meanings to different cultures such as the Goddess Belief, Ancient Greek Belief, Native Belief and Metaphysical Belief. Basic Moon names are: January—Wild Animal Moon: February—Snow Moon: March—Thaw Moon: April—Shower Moon: May—Flower Moon: June—Strawberry Moon: July—Thunder Moon: August—Red Moon: September—Harvest Moon: October—Hunter Moon: November—Rest Moon: December—Cold Moon.

MOONSTONE—a milky-sheen colored mineral used to provide one with the riches of the universe.

MORPHOGENETIC FIELDS—fields that are present throughout the universe which guide the development of spiritual information for those who desire it.

MOSANDRITE—
crystals with a wide range of colors used to enhance the gift of prophecy and psychic knowledge.

MOTHER—the second aspect of the Goddess. The bearer of all things. The subconscious mind.

MOUNTAIN ASH—Scandinavian's believe this to be the best wood for making dowsing rods.

MOUNTAINS—indicates the ups and downs of one's chosen path. Wisdom and understanding.

MOUNT SHASTA—believed to be a highly spiritual place which became a sacred site for the area Native Americans. It has become a unique center of activity for the Metaphysical movement.

MOXIBUSTION—the aim here is directed at the tsubos. The healer uses a small piece of herb which is ignited and generally allowed to burn down to the skin. See tsubos.

M.S.P.—mind sensory perception. A system of mental perception that is similar to ESP, but works with heightened sensory perception rather than images or thoughts.

MU—the lost continent of Lemuria. The continent prior to Atlantis. see Lemuria.

MUHAMMAD—a medium of God and the Prophet of Islam. (as Jesus is to Christianity)

MUCUSLESS DIET HEALING —the belief that there is only one disease in all humanity, that of constipation brought on by bad or improper eating habits. The answer is extended fasting to cleanse the body, followed by a diet of raw and cooked vegetables, as well as any vegetables or food which do not produce mucus. Highly advanced spiritual people follow this diet today.

MULLITE—pale pink minerals used in psychic phenomenon to stimulate the transfer of spiritual laws from other worlds.

MULTIDIMENSIONAL PERSONALITIES—the belief that one entity has or uses the same soul for many different personalities. i.e. one life experience in this reality, another life experience in another world or universe. Two or more existence's at one time.

MULTIDEMSIONAL REALITIES—the belief that one lives in many existence's at one time.

MULTIPLE PERSONALITIES—a state in which multiple personalities exist in one physical body.

MULTITUDINOUS DEATHS—the ongoing death of the atoms, cells and molecules of the body. A complete new body is formed every seven years. The Metaphysical belief that, one is one's own creator, is associated with these deaths. see multitudinous rebirths.

MULTITUDINOS REBIRTHS—the continual rebirth of cells, atoms and molecules as they continually die, i.e. hair and fingernails. see multitudinous deaths.

MUSCLE READING—finding a hidden object by watching the subtle muscular clues of the one who knows it is located or hidden. see cumberlandism.

MUSIC CHANNELLED—music received from the psychic realm through channelling. Narada records publishes channeled music only.

MUSIC TELEKINETICALLY PRODUCED—an instrument that produces music without the aid of a person, such as a piano playing on its own or a horn that begins to play by itself.

MUSIC THERAPY—the use of music as a means of communicating with other persons whose communication skills are weak, such as those who cannot speak or autistic persons.

MUTABLE—in Astrology, one of the three modes of signs: changeable, responsive, and flowing. The mutable signs are Gemini, Virgo, Sagittarius and Pisces.

MYSTERIES—secret religious cults of the Hellenistic period that needed complete confidence in their members to keep their rituals, practices and beliefs completely secret and out of the reach of the people. A strong belief on the Goddess and the preservation of everlasting life. Carl Jung worked with the ancient Mysteries.

MYSTERY RELIGIONS—a spiritual and religious group or culture, in the Mediterranean World during the Hellenistic period who believed on securing the goodwill of the Gods in this life, rather than seeking a place in the hereafter.

MYSTIC—one who is able to understand things beyond all physical knowledge. Knowledge of the spiritual realm and how to use spiritual energy.

MYSTICAL EXPERIENCE—(spiritual experience) an event or happening unexplainable to the conscious mind, generally of a positive nature. A sudden knowing without learning.

MYSTICISM—the direct awareness of God through the self. A belief that the Deity is all pervading. A belief on the supernatural.

MYTH— many meanings. Stories of historical events that serve to unfold a world view of a people, or explain a practice, belief or natural phenomenon. Maps to Spiritual understanding.

MYTHOLOGY—the study of myths. Stories that explain the creation of the cosmos.

N

NADIR—in Astrology, the point farthest below the local horizon, the approximate position of the sun at midnight, the cusp of the fourth house, the fourth house as a whole.

NAIAD FIELD—the electromagnetic energy field which holds the emotional imprints of a thought-form and the vibratory frequency of each and every thing. The field which makes all forms of ESP and parapsychology possible

NADORITE—brown to yellow crystals used to assist one leave the body in "out-of-body travel".

NAMING—a given name during the ritual of Christening and spiritual offerings. Not the name given to a child at birth. Different beliefs have specific ages for this ritual to take place. A second parent is also appointed.

NATURAL CHANNEL—one who, without special training, has the ability and access to all psychic input, i.e. precognition, medium and healing.

NATURAL LAW—that set of laws set forth in the beginning, by God or the Deity, as the working basis of all creation, without which no manifestation can occur or exist.

NATURAL PHILOSOPHERS—a name given to the philosophers of antiquity, whose main concern was phenomena and physics such as light, heat, energy and sound, rather than the actual structure of physical matter.

NATURE LANGUAGE—speaking in an unknown language believed to be the original language of humankind. see xenoglossis.

NATURE SPIRITS—types of entities or spirits believed to live in the Nature world, they possess super powers and are usually invisible to human beings. see nature religion.

NATUROPATHY—a form of health and healing attained by using natural methods such as diet, fasting, cleansing and massage.

NATAL HOROSCOPE—a chart showing one's horoscope for the exact moment of birth.

NATIVE OF—the one about whom the astrologer is speaking. i.e. a person born under Taurus is considered to be a native of Taurus.

NATURAL LAW—laws or patterns set into motion by the Divinity which humankind works with to their benefit, or against to their eventual detriment.

NATURAL MAGIC— the application of ESP or Universal powers, usually for healing purposes, without the use of spells, incantations or other instruments.

NATURE RELIGION—a world belief on Nature as a way of life. An observation of life in a natural and mystical experience. see nature spirits.

NATURE SPIRIT—a spirit which oversees and aids the networking of nature and its ecological balance.

NATUROPATH—one who practices Naturopathic medicine.

NATUROPATHIC MEDICINE—a holistic approach to health. Promotes health through use of natural agents and processes.

NAZCA LINES—giant lines, geometric figures, human and animal drawings on the dessert mesa near the village of Nazca in Peru. Believed to be the work of space beings, however their purpose and arrival is unknown. Believed to be the landing strips of space crafts.

NEAR DEATH EXPERIENCE—the separation of the soul from the body in times of extreme illness or danger. A sensation described as travelling down a tunnel accompanied by a feeling of great happiness.

NECROMANCY—the art of foretelling the future by contacting the dead.

NEGATIVE—many meanings. A natural polarity which is passive, static, receptive and nurturing. It complements the positive polarity which is active, creative and dynamic. Evil thoughts or energies.

NEGATIVE CAPABILITY—a term the poet Keats used to describe a state of mind that can accept ambiguity, being able to live with unquestioned facts, reasons and mysteries.

NEGATIVE GREEN ENERGY—the counter-clockwise energy which spirals downward inside a pyramid and preserves and dehydrates that which it contacts.

NEO-PAGANISM—a modern movement which began in the 1960's primarily concerned with revived and reconstructed pre-Christian nature religions and mystery traditions. Included in Neo-Paganism are the occult, environmentalists, spiritual awareness, mythology and Goddess belief.

NEPHELINE—a wide range of colored crystals used to enhance rebirthing.

NERVES—the channels through which information is carried both to and from the central station of the physical brain.

NETWORKING—linking individual knowledge and spiritual awareness together to become more conscious of the complete spiritual realm.

NEURYPNOLOGY—the ancient word for hypnotism.

NEUTRAL MAGNETIC—a magnet with both poles potentized used to find energy problems of the Aura caused by blockage. Also used by Homeopathic practitioners.

NEW AGE— controversial term applied to spiritual and social movements such as new religions, mysticism, psychology, occult, ecology and parapsychology. New-something without precedence, something about to be formed. Age-a cycle of time which is dominated by a specific quality. i.e. stone age. Teachings of new and spiritually higher beliefs of self and deity. Leaving the age of Pisces and entering the age of Aquarius. Belief on reincarnation.

NEW AGE GOD—a fundamental change of consciousness in that one creates one's own reality, yet knows "All that Is." A moving out of the belief that one is separate from God to a consciousness that one is united and at one with God. see all that is.

NEW AGE MAN/WOMAN—one who feels at onement with All That Is or the Deity. A strong understanding that one is a co-creator with God.

NEW BRAIN—a term used to designate the cerebrum. Called "new" because it is developed relatively recently in the course of evolution. The spiritual extension of the brain in the Aquarium age. see old brain.

NEW THOUGHT MOVEMENT—the art of clearing one's mind of one belief and beginning another. see mind cure.

NEXT PLANE OF LIFE—the next level of reality. When one has completed all the necessary lives required to complete this realities chosen experiences.

NICTALOPES—persons who have the ability to see in the dark but must keep their eyes covered or stay indoors during the day. All mediums are believed to have some degree of nictalopes.

NIGHT—symbol of the subconscious. Negative energy. The realm of the Goddess.

NIGHT FLIGHT—a slang name given to witches with the assumption that witches can fly through the air on various crafts such as broomsticks.

NIGHTMARE—fear in the dream state caused by images arising from the subconscious mind.

NINE—symbol of completion, attainment, success, a step to new beginnings and spiritual advancement to another plane or level.

NIRVANA—a Hindu and Buddhist belief that one has excluded all earthly desires and possessions, then continues to grow along spiritual paths.

NOBLE EIGHT-FOLD PATH—the path of an adept. One must be capable of noble or perfect understanding of aspiration, speech, action, daily living, mindfulness, effort and absorption.

NON-PHYSICAL—an entity or soul without a physical body. The realm of the spirit.

NORTHUPITE—yellow to gray-brown crystals which are used as protection when travelling out of the body.

NOSTRADAMUS—the Latinized name of Michael de Nostredame (1503-66) a doctor who performed remarkable cures. He became famous for his prophesies expressed in pure quatrains, some of which are to come true in the 19th and 20th centuries, some of his 1000 predictions are to come about in

3797. Scholars have said that half of his predictions have come true.

NOUMENON—the informationless area of existence, energy and awareness.

NOVEMBER MOON—known as the Rest Moon. A time for spiritual reflection and of giving thanks for the harvest. see Rest Moon.

NUMBERS—Pythagorus is believed to have been the first to understand that numbers constitute the true nature of all reality. Ancient beliefs were that odd numbers were sacred to the Goddesses and even numbers were sacred to the Gods.

NUMEROLOGY—an analysis of the hidden meaning of numbers. A study of numbers and how they affect our daily spiritual and physical lives. A belief that numbers have vibrations, that it is the vibration that influences, not the number. A concept that the universe is constructed in a mathematical pattern.

NUUMMIT—dark colored crystal used to promote energy flow throughout the body, clears any energy blockage.

NYMPHS—water beings who control birth and fertility, dissolution and death. Entities that live in both the physical and astral realms.

O

OAHSPE—referred to as the New Age or Metaphysical Bible which was channeled in 1882 by John Newbrough and consisted of 1000 pages. This book speaks of the human race evolving from the continent of Pan whis is similar to the lost continent of Lemuria. It records history 78000 years prior to the birth of Christ.

OAK—symbol of the Goddess Diana. Strength and long life.

OBEAH—the art of African sorcery which combines Voodoo and Christianity.

OBJECTIVE—the outer physical world. See subjective.

OBJECTIVE REALITY—that which is created by the conscious mind. Physical reality. Consciousness of the outer physical world.

OBJECTIVE MIND—that part of the mind which operates in the outer or material world. This mind must be selfish to preserve the physical body which houses the soul. i.e. fight or flight.

OBSCURE NIGHT — a belief of the Ancient Essenes that prior to ones enlightenment, one must look at oneself and see that which one does not like. This moment was referred to as the Obscure Night. A time of personal adjustment.

OBSERVATIONAL THEORY—the theory that Psi is brought about by the Psi source observing the result of its observation.see psi

OBSESSION—an invasion of a living person by a discarnate spirit creating a complete displacement of one's personality. see possession.

OBSIDIAN—many colors, a volcanic glass used as a shield against negativity and which assists in changing negativity to positivety.

OCCAM'S RAZOR—a philosophic principle which states that it is best to work through all likely solutions of a problem, before approaching magical solutions.

OCCULT—a belief in the supernatural, paranormal forces and beings. A belief that has hidden or secret beliefs. Mysterious. Some believe this to be the Esoteric Science. Science of the soul.

OCCULT HIERARCHY—spiritual beings on the inner planes of the solar system divided into twelve levels or hierarchies consisting of chohans, adepts and initiates. see chohans, adepts and initiates.

OCCULTIST—one who believes and practices the occult.

OCTOBER MOON—known as the Hunter's Moon. This is the month that the winter food is hunted and stored for the winter months. see Hunter's Moon.

ODIC FORCE—named after the German God Odin, a universal force first recorded by Baron Von Reichenbach in 1851 which signifies an all pervading power. God. Known as the OD force.

ODOUR OF SANCTITY—a scent provided by the Deity or God at seances and gatherings which assist in good health. Mediums will produce psychic scents given by the Deity which are necessary for those present. see perfumes.

OFF THE GRID—a Metaphysical term meaning living in nature. Living without power or gas.

OINTMENT—Witchcraft ritual where any substance is rubbed on the skin to produce magical results. Used on the third eye to enhance psychic visions.

OKENITE—white blade-shaped crystals used to give one the feeling of being "at home" within oneself.

OLD BRAIN—the lower portion of the brain that developed relatively early in the course of evolution, responsible for bodily functions. see new brain.

OLD SOUL—a soul which has incarnated into the physical reality many times. One who may be without karma and has chosen to incarnate to the physical reality for "helping" purposes. see young soul.

OLD WO/MAN—symbol of the collective unconsciousness. Age old wisdom.

OLD WOMAN—the crone aspect of the Goddess.

OM—a sound from the Eastern beliefs. A chant often used at the beginning or end of a meditation.Often chanted at most spiritual gatherings. A power word.

OMEGA—the end. Used in most religious and spiritual dogma, Alpha and Omega meaning the beginning and the end. The last letter of the Greek alphabet.

OMEN—a sign believed to give information regarding direction or future events.

OMNIPOTENT—all powerful. Unlimited God power. The quality of having unlimited power and knowledge.

OMNISCIENT—knowing all things. Having infinite awareness, understanding and insight.

ONE—the beginning of all realities. The prime number from which all others evolve. The oneness. The beginning of creativity waiting for two or balance.

ONE ARM DOWSING—dowsing by rigidly extending one arm straight out, shoulder high. A dowsing response is indicated when the arm rises three or four inches.

ONENESS— no real separation. Everything that lives within a unified field of being. i.e. middle C on a piano, all other C's are the same but different.

ONTOLOGY—the study of the nature of being and the living reality.

ONYZ—a variety of colored chalcedony-type minerals, black is used to banish or absorb grief.

OPAL—a wide range of colors, used to enhance faithfulness in love relationships.

OPEN CHANNEL—a direct connection between a medium and the deity, or spirit when communication is taking place.

OPPOSITION—in Astrology, an aspect characterized by a 180 degree separation between two planets, symbolizing the process of polarization or tension.

OPTIMUM—the greatest and best of a situation or event. Being exactly where one wants to be in both the physical and spiritual realms.

ORACLE—a place or person who is used by the universe or Deity to give messages or answers to those searching for direction. Universal or spiritual messages that need to be delivered to one without request.

ORACULAR TREES—trees with oracles and pronouncements connected to ancient Mythology such as The Whispering Oaks of Dodona and The Laurel Oracle of Apollo at Delphi.

ORANGE LIGHT—(energy) color of the belly charka. Second colour of the rainbow. Color used to heal the belly area. Used to push objects away from oneself in the practice of telekinesis.

ORB—in Astrology, the limits of tolerance within which an aspect is considered functional. Variable and subjective, but usually taken to be about seven degrees.

ORDER OF THE GOLDEN DAWN—founded in 1888 in London by MacGregor Mathers. A secret society which received its direction, while he was in trance, from "Secret Chiefs" and "Masters". The order broke up in 1990 with little known knowledge of it.

ORGANISM—a plant, animal or entity that has two or more parts working together to maintain life.

ORISHA—African Deity similar to a Christian Saint.

ORPHEUS—a legendary Greek singer of hymns who founded the religion "Orphism". It is believed that he attracted animals and stones with his charms.

ORTHOCLASE—minerals used to promote happiness and pleasantness.

OSUN—a small metal rooster who, according to the Santeria belief system is the guardian of all homes.

OTHER SIDE—a place where spirits go after physical death. Spiritual realm. Home of spiritual guides.

OTHER WORLD—the basic idea that there are more spiritual "other worlds" existing along side our normal world. Another term for dimensions, levels and existences.

OUIJA BOARD—a board bearing the letters of the alphabet used to spell out messages from spiritual entities, activated by the fingers of mediums.

OUTER EGO—that which enables one to manipulate the world in which one exists.

OUT OF BODY EXPERIENCE—the soul's temporary departure from the physical body.

OVERALL IDENTITY—the soul or spirit that oversees more than one physical body. A spirit choice of a networking reality.

OVERSELF—the soul or spirit part of our reality. The real "I". The whole power source with knowledge of all incarnations. see higher self.

OWL—many meanings. An Egyptian symbol of death. Night and cold. A Greek symbol of wisdom and knowledge. The staring eyes connect it to the Eye Goddesses.

OWYHEEITE—silver to white needle-like crystals used to acquire wisdom.

P

PALLADIUM—silver-white metallic mineral used extensively in psychic healing.

PALM—the flat part of one's hand. The concave part of the hand at the base of the fingers and thumb which is used in palmistry.

PALO—an Afro-Cuban spiritual-magic in which human remains, taken from graves with permission of the dead, are used in rituals. A sect based on the beliefs and magic of the African Kong tribe.

PALLOMANCY—Afro-Cuban form of divination. Divination with the use of a pendulum. see pendulum. see palo.

PALM'S PSYCHIC CHAKRA—the hand chakra is located in the center of the palm. The "cup" area of the palm.

PALMISTRY—the study of using the hands, palms and the lines of the palms to give direction to one's life. A form of reading the future.

PANENTHEISM—a belief that the Deity includes the world as part of, rather than the whole of, it's being. The belief that the Deity is more than the sum of it's parts.

PANTHEISM—a doctrine that identifies God with the entire universe, every particle being part of him/her. A belief that everything existing creates a unity and that this unity is divine. A belief that denies the personality of God and equates God with the forces and laws of the universe.

PANTOMNESIA—a regression of the memory. The feeling that a thing experienced has been seen before. see deja vu.

PAPAGOITE—sky blue crystals within crystals

used as a calming or tranquillizing energy.

PARACELSIAN—large colorless crystals used in the work of alchemy. see paracelsus.

PARACELSUS—(1493-1541) a Swiss alchemist and philosopher who believed in natural magic, the existence of the aura and the holistic approach to healing. see paracelsian.

PARADOX—a logical contradiction for both God and man.

PARAKINESIS—a movement of objects with little physical contact or exertion, such as lightly touching a heavy object and it easily moves.

PARALLELISM—a dualistic belief that mind and matter are synchronized without acting upon each other.

PARALLEL LIFE—a state where the same soul simultaneously incarnates into different bodies, often at great distances from each other. Each body, or parrell life, then experiences all of the other bodies experiences.

PARAMNESIA—a distortion of recognition or memory. A form of deja vu.

PARANORMAL—beyond normal experience. Events unexplainable by rational or scientific means. In many cases science is now close to believing many paranormal theories.

PARANORMAL COGNITION—another term for psychic phenomenon or ESP. see ESP.

PARAPHYSICS—a study of the energies or forces involved in paranormal events such as ESP, dowsing and psychokinesis.

PARAPSYCHOLOGY—a scientific study outside of psychology which includes extrasensory perception, telepathy and telekinesis. Another name for psychical research. See psychotronics.

PARENTAL CHOICE—a soul, prior to entering the physical body, chooses its parents to complete it's chosen life plan. see life plan.

PARTNERSHIP—the acceptance and working together with God for the good of everything and everyone.

PASSAGE OF MATTER THROUGH MATTER—the ability to pass through matter, such as walls, by dematerialization and materialization. see apport and teleportation.

PASSIVE INTELLIGENCE—the part of the intelligence which disappears at death with the physical body. Non spiritual intelligence, fictional information. see active intelligence.

PAST LIFE—the physical and spiritual life one has lived and experienced during a previous incarnation.

PAST LIFE RECALL—can be achieved by hypnosis, induction and on occasion by instant visions, feelings etc. Memories of Past lives.

PAST LIFE THERAPY—therapy which includes experiencing past lives to enhance spiritual growth. A therapy to experience after death and before birth.

PAST LIFE INFLUENCES—in this physical reality lives are linear and affect one another creating cause and effect. In the spiritual reality all lives happen at once, therefore all lives interact without creating karma. Cause and effect only applies in the physical realm. see past personalities.

PAST PERSONALITIES—memories of events, actions and karma from past lifetimes which influence the personality of this lifetime.

PATH—one's chosen physical life experience, chosen in the spirit state prior to birth. A way to Spiritual growth.

PAWANG—an African dowsing rod made of segmented rattan rod, with seeds or beads inside so that it rattles when a response is found.

PEACE—having pleasant thoughts and feelings.

PEACE PROFOUND—a state of mind which allows one to face all changing conditions with a philosophic, spiritual and detached attitude.

PEARL—a wide range of colors used to enhance innocence. A Moslem symbol of Heaven. The sacred center.

PECOS DIAMOND—a form of rose colored crystals used by the young and young at heart for a feeling of joy and well-being.

PEGASUS—a Northern Constellation near the vernal equinoctial point. Converting evil into good, as in the myth of his creation, where he sprang from the blood of Medusa when Perseus cut of her head. Used in Astrology.

PENDULUM—an object suspended from a fixed point which freely swings back and forth Used to answer questions that require yes, no or a neutral answer.

PENDY—a nickname for pendulum, most often used with map dowsing.

PENETRATIVE CLAIRVOYANCE—the ability to see through solid objects such as walls and fences. see x-ray vision.

PENTAGRAM—a five pointed star used in most magic rituals. Frequently identified with Wicca.

PENTACLE—a five pointed star with one point up. Star of David. One of the four suits of the Tarot, indicating finances and growth.

Symbol of the Goddess in all her forms.

PERCEPTION—an intuitive thought of knowing and understanding. The phenomenon of knowing something without the use of normal channels to gain this knowledge.

PERCIPIENT—one in an ESP tests who attempts to guess another's thoughts, identify objects or events.

PERFUMES—certain illnesses give off certain scents, mediums believe this to be the body trying to heal itself by showing one what it lacks.

PERICLASE—colorless to white crystals used to assist in depression by taking on the depression.

PERIPHEAL—the outer or side view of one's vision said to be the area of the visual manifestation of spiritual beings or objects.

PERISPIRIT—another term for the spiritual body.

PERMANENT MAGNETISM—magnetism which is due to a molecular magnetomotive force from the unbalanced spin of orbiting electrons.

PERSON—a spiritual being with a physical body which thinks, feels, has self-consciousness and self-determination. A human being.

PERSONA THEORY—a hypothesis by Hart that spirits of the dead, and mediums, are temporary re-creations of the personality structures (personas) of the spirit by the subconscious of the active medium. However the active medium may be speaking to a helpful spirit.

PERSONALITY—a gestalt of ever-changing perceptions. That part of a person which makes one either likable or unlikable. The portion of one which expresses the spiritual character of the soul.

PERSONATION—a temporary possession of one's body by an alien entity with the person being aware of the possession.

PERVADING—throughout the entire being. All knowing. Totally accepted.

PETOSKEY STONE—a fossilized coral with an inner marking resembling an eye. The coral is gray-white and the eye is white. Used to ward off evil and the curse of the "evil eye."see evil eye.

PETRA—stones used as a means of communicating with the Ancients, Spiritual Masters or the Divinity. Received in 1982 by Sofia Nina.

PETRIFIED WOOD—ancient wood turned into stone, used for strength in all areas of one's life.

PHALLUS—(penis)male energy in the act of creation.

PHANTOM—an apparition or ghost.

PHANTOM CRYSTAL—a crystal with another crystal grown up into itself.

PHENACITE—yellow, brown and red crystals promoting deep meditation and inner "knowing of all things."

PHENOMENON—something witnessed by the senses that cannot be explained in a material way. Unexplainable in this physical reality.

PHILIP—an artificial poltergeist created by the Toronto Society for Psychical Research, created to show how intense concentration can create real spirits.

PHILOSOPHER'S STONE—the substance by which base metals can be turned into gold. The substance which transmits perfect qualities. The spiritual gnosis and exalted wisdom whose virtue transmutes one to a higher plane of consciousness and personal power.

PHOENIX—a mythological bird which lived for 500 years, burned itself to ashes on a pyre and rose alive from the ashes to live another lifetime. Reincarnation. Rebirth. A symbol of the Sun Gods.

PHONE CALLS FROM THE DEAD—normal calls from the dead, usually one with whom the recipient had a close relationship. Actress Ida Lupino received a call from her father, six months after he died, to tell her where he had left some documents. Several such calls have been recorded.

PHONE-VOYANCE—a form of psychic television where the persons talking on the phone are able to see the entire room and its occupants as if it was on television.

PHOSPHORESCENT-LIKE GLOW—The aura glow. The ability to see the electromagnetic structures that compose molecules. A spiritual presence.

PHRENOLOGY—the study of the bumps on the head from which character traits can be read. A form of divination using the twenty six areas or bumps on the head.

PHYSICAL PHENOMENON—the actual touching of a spirit, ghost or apparition. Usually harmless.

PHYSICAL REALITY—that which one sees with the physical eye. The reality of the present existence in the physical world.

PHYSIOLOGY—study of the physical body, how its organisms work and how they are achieved.

PHRENOLOGY—an art of divination which uses the shape of the skull as the medium of interpretation.

PHYSIOGNOMY—the art of divination by the use of some part of the physical body such as the face, palm or eyes.

PICO DELLA MIRANDOLA—a 15th century philosopher who wrote "heptaplus," the Cabbalist account of creation. He wrote many other books including a book discrediting Astrology.

PIETRO d'ABANO—a 13th century philosopher and doctor of medicine whose modern views collided with the church. He was the first person to deny the existence of satan, the devil and negative energies.

PIEZOELECTRIC—a form of electricity or energy produced by applying pressure on a substance that changes its shape and then returns to its original shape, as in crystals.

PILGRIM—the seeker of knew and hidden knowledge. Journey men of new areas. Those who enter new territory. Spiritual seekers.

PILGRIM'S WAY—a system of directional or "way" locations across the universe which provide a path of awareness where the enlightened are able to gain experience and elevation by the presence of the Spiritual Pilgrims.

PINAKIOLITE—black metallic tabular crystals used in finding the solutions to Ancient Mysteries.

PI-RAY ENEGRY—an energy neither positive or negative, called "the ray of life" by the Ancient Egyptians. Used in pyramids to filter out the green energy. Sunlight amplifies pi-ray energy and pi-ray energy amplifies consciousness. A purifying energy. see green energy.

PISCES—the Zodiac sign (the fishes) February 19-March 20.

PLACEMENT TEST—the ability to move object, with the mind, to the exact

requested position.
PLAIT—a braid used in magic made of knots and ropes.
PLANCHETTE—apparatus for receiving information from the other side. Similar to a Ouija Board. This board has a pencil attached and moves on castors over a blank piece of paper. It writes messages without the help of a physical being.
PLANE—A state of consciousness within the greater consciousness. The universe is divided into seven planes, each plane having seven subplanes, each plane and subplane having its own entity for spiritual assistance to humankind. A place one goes to upon leaving the physical body. Used as a division of planes in the spiritual realm. i.e. etheric and astral planes.
PLANET—different cosmic energies. One of the many physical object in this or other universe's. In Astrology, any celestial body that moves through the zodiac in a predictable way. Astrologically the term includes the sun and the moon. The Earth is a planet.
PLANETARY CONSCIOUSNESS—born out of the ecology movement of the 1960's, and expanded with the concept that the earth is a growing living self-regulating organism.
PLANETARY LOGOS—the highest planetary spirit. The God of the planet. see Logos.
PLANETARY TRAVEL—the first psychical planetary travel was recorded in 1813 when German Dr. F Romer travelled to the moon and all the planets.
PLANTING SEEDS—a statement made by one person to another, to try to influence the other person into a particular spiritual

direction. A belief that one's subconscious mind acts on everything it hears.

PLANTS(psychicism of)— the Ancients believed that plants had spirits and possessed magical powers. Modern day science has tried many experiments with inconclusive results.

PLASTICS— supernaturally obtained imprints and moulds, made by spiritual beings leaving prints in flower dust or any substance that will show an imprint. Many such experiments took place in England in the 1920's.

PLATINUM—steel-gray grains of minerals which aid in providing permanence of relationships.

PLEIADES—a cluster of stars in the constellation Taurus which is believed to be the home or living place of most extraterrestrials.

PLINY—(24-79 A.D.) a Roman polymath who wrote the "Natural History," one of the first to write on the benefits of Naturopathic medicines. see holistic health.

PLUS 1 (+1)—a mental telepathy test where one hits on the upcoming target or item.

PLUTONIFICATION—in Astronomy, an introspect made by one's Pluto to any point on another's chart, symbolizing the penetration and transpersonalization or the corruption and domination of the affected point.

POLARIA—an extinct West Slavic language, (Polabian) and people, of the Baltic Coast which was the home of the first Root Race. see first Root Race.

POLARITY—an electrical or magnetic force possessed by all manifestation of creation, having a character of negative or positive. see negative and positive energy.

POLARITY CHAKRA—another term for charka. Balancing chakra.

POLARITY THERAPY—a form of healing by stimulating the charge of polar opposites of one's body. see magnetic healing.

POLARIZATION—a centering or balancing of the energies of the physical body.

POLTERGISTS—a German word for a noisy racketing, possibly destructive spirit. Generally energies that are unable to receive the attention necessary to fulfill their journeys. If not attended they may begin to move or throw objects. see poltergeist medium.

POLTERGIST MEDIUM—one who appears to be the focal point of a poltergeist outbreak, in most cases a teenager with inner angers.

POLYTHEISM—the concept of many Gods.

POLYGRAPH—an instrument used in psychic research which records electrical potential generated by brain waves, eye movement and muscular tension.

POMEGRANTES—an ancient belief that symbolizes the female, passive aspects of life. Connected with the underworld Queen and often called the fruit of the dead. The Greeks believed it sprang from the blood of Dionysus.

POPPET—another term for the wax doll used in voodoo.

PORTENT—a sign of what is to come. An omen. A vision of either positive or negative events.

POSITIVE GREEN ENERGY—the clockwise rotating energy which rises from the top of a pyramid, also given off by living plants. It gives vitality to all living things. see negative green energy.

POSSESSION—the apparent occupation, of the mind of a person, by a spirit. Generally unwanted and trouble some. see obsession.

POST COGNITION—knowledge of an event or situation soon after its happening. see retro cognition.

POSTULANT—one who has a desire to advance spiritually but does not have the financial means to do so, and must work or commit oneself to certain responsibilities.

POTENTIZE—to energize or endow with power.

POTION—a witch's mixture of liquids, roots, insects and animals. Drink of immortality. A dose of liquid.

POWER—better described as "use of energy." The more knowledgeable as to the use of energy, the more power one has.

POWER BAG—a Shaman's source of power. A container with stones, crystals, animal bits, rattles and other energy endowed objects used for healing or divination. see medicine bag.

POWER POINT—locations, sites, or objects believed to have more magical and supernatural energies than others. Usually Ancient sites with megaliths.

POWER HOUSE—powerful centers of transmutation established by the Ancients of Shamballa. see centers of transmutation.

PRALAYA—a Sanskrit word for the time between incarnations. see soul choice time.

PRANA—a Sanskrit word for life breath.

PRAYER—speaking or asking God for help and direction. Talking to the Dieties. A petition.

PRECIPITATION—a deposit, in one's body, of psychic and etheric charges from a past life. i.e. bad karma and perverse practices.

PRECOGNITION—an unexplainable knowledge of future events. A spiritual giving of events about to happen. A knowing of a event prior to its happening.

PRECOGNITIVE TELEPATHY—extrasensory awareness of another person's future mental content or state.

PREDESTINATION—fate. A belief that everything is laid out for us in this lifetime, that we have no choices.

PREDICTION—a statement of future events with the knowledge of precognition, something to happen in the future. A prophecy in which future information is obtained through psychic means.

PRE-EXISTENCE—a term meaning that we have lived before this existence. Reincarnation. Prior to entering the physical body.

PREMONITION—a type of prophecy that is a forewarning of a future event. The knowledge of a future event, either positive or negative.

PRESENCE—spirits that work within this reality for the purpose of helping individuals. A feeling or knowing that a spirit form is near.

PRESENT EXISTANCE—the life or reality in which one now lives.

PRESENTIMENT—foreboding, a premonition of something to come which is undesirable. A personal premonition of future events.

PREVISION—events of the future acquired in vision form.

PRIEST—a highly trained person in organized religions who is responsible for other's spiritual growth.

PRINCE—a symbol of one level below the top. Not yet arrived spiritually.

PRIMAL TRIAD—in Astrology, the sun moon and ascendant taken together as the skeleton of the individuality.

PROGRAM—a set of rules and activities which guide or direct spiritual energy.

PROGRESSION—experiencing the future of this life or a coming life. Growth or advancement. In Astrology, any of the number of synthetic predictive techniques in which planets are made to move through one's birthchart at varying rates.

PROJECTION—the freeing, or sending, of the psychic body into time and space, generally made to attract or help another.

PROJECTIVE ENERGY—positive, strong energy that is put forward, projected outward and away from one, as in healing or psychic assistance. see receptive energy.

PROMETHEUS—according to Greek Mythology, Prometheus made man out of clay, then Athena breathed life into these images, creating humankind.

PROPHECY—spiritual wisdom. Stating of events that are yet to happen, sometime believed to be divinely inspired.

PROPHET—one who speaks on God's behalf. An Initiate. One who spends his life studying spirituality and the events yet to come. One who creates prophecy. see prophecy.

PROTECTION—a request from the deity, by either prayer or visualization, to have a white light surround one-self for protection from psychic attack. Spiritual protection from unethical practising psychics. see shield.

PROXY SITTING—a sitting with a medium, where the person desiring to receive information from the spirits is represented by someone else.

PSEUDOFORM—a thought projection of oneself of which one is not aware. Often seen in the astral realm. see secondary constructions.

PSEUDO-OBSESSION—an obsession of a personality from a past life, especially when one passes over or dies before their time. The ghost like figure of a physical body that has died but the spirit is not yet ready to leave.

PSI—the mysterious factor behind all ESP actions. The root cause of the ability to perform ESP. Scientific word for unknown energy factor. Some believe this energy to be the Divinity. The symbol in quantum mechanics for a wave factor.

PSILOMELANE—deep-gray to black minerals used to re-direct excess energy.

PSIOLOGY—the study of parapsychology. Psychical research or the study of the Divine.

PSIONIC MEDICINE— a medical diagnos is done by dowsing, and the treatment is by psychic means.

PSYCHE—ancient Greek word for Soul. The human spirit.

PSYCHIC—one who is sensitive to non-physical forces. One who is able to contact the world of spirit. One who perceives through means other than the five senses.

PSYCHIC ARCHAEOLOGY—the art of archaeologists with psychic abilities in psychometry. Handling objects or artifacts, and receiving messages from the object as to its date etc. A highly controversial art.

PSYCHIC ATTACK—a paranormal attack on one which causes physical and mental stress or illness, caused by one believing that this attack is possible. Methods used in psychic attack are voodoo, sorcery, demons and thought forms. Impossible to occur if one believes that it will not occur. see evil eye.

PSYCHIC BODY—an aggregate of the more higher, sensitive levels of consciousness permeating man's being. An energy field which corresponds to the physical body.

PSYCHIC CRIMINOLOGY—the use of psychics during investigations.

PSYCHIC CURRENTS—the channels or "roads" between levels of reality. A means of inter-reality travel.

PSYCHIC ENERGY—an energy which operates without muscular contact or connection. Action at a distance causing visible motion and audible sounds from a solid substance.

PSYCHIC ETHER—hypothetical substantial substance or energy which propagates thought waves, records impressions of events and produces corresponding patterns.

PSYCHIC EXPERIENCE— an experience related to the psychic or higher levels of consciousness, coming from either man or God. An experience unexplainable through the physical five senses. A paranormal experience.

PSYHIC FORCE—a force without muscular connection which causes an action at a distance, believed to be the Odin or God force. see psychic energy.

PSYCHIC HEALER—one who cures illness with the help of the Divinity through thought waves or the laying on of hands.

PSYCHIC IMPRINTS—see plastics.

PSYCHIC MIND—that which is working when one receives psychic impulses. Psychic mind is at work when one sleep or dreams. One's direct link with the inner self, the universe, god or the deity.

PSYCHIC MOULDS—see plastics.

PSYCHIC MUSEUM—a museum which contains automatic writings, automatic drawings and manifestations. Established in England in 1925.

PSYCHIC MUSIC—instruments which play without the help of any persons. Music heard without the use of instruments.

PSYCHIC PHOTOGRAPHY—the appearance of images or objects on ones film or photos not normally in view of the physical five senses.

PSYCHIC PLANE—the meeting place or field of psychic bodies that have left the physical reality. The plane where we, in spirit state, work for the uplifting of mankind. The plane from which one receives psychic messages.

PSYCHIC READING—a sitting with a medium with psychic abilities to receive psychic answers to questions. Answers received from non-physical forces.

PSYCHIC SCIENCE—a system of facts to demonstrate the existence of spirits outside of the body, and their ability to communicate with humanity.

PSYCHIC SOUNDS—sounds which are heard without anyone speaking or making sounds.

PSYCHIC SURGERY—the alleged power of one to

perform physical surgery with the bare hands and without the use of anaesthetic. Surgery completed on the Aura or Etheric Body which in turn heals the physical body. Believed to be common in the Philippines.

PSYCHIC TOUCHES—being touched by something when no-one is near or close-by, usually a good omen or caution.

PSYCHIC WARP—an opening or door. A line in universal energy where one is able to connect oneself with other universes of experience. Realities where symbols come to life and thoughts are not denied their potential.

PSYCHICAL—psychic or paranormal.

PHYCHICAL RESEARCH—original term used for what is now called parapsychology.

PSYCHISM—a term used to denote every kind of phenomena. Including those of mediumship, sensitiveness and hypnosis.

PSYCHOANALYSIS—an analysis performed using free association, dreams, emotions and blunders to reveal subconscious or spiritual functions and conflicts.

PSYCHOBOLY—a term used in psychokinesis, especially when used for wrong or evil purposes as in the "evil-eye" phenomenon. see evil eye.

PSYCHODRAMA—the visualization of some psychological tension in the form of a drama or story. Many dreams and nightmares are psycho dramatic.

PSYCHODYNAMICALLY OPEN CHAKRAS—a well balanced, receiving and sending open, clean chakra.

PSYCHOENERGETICS—a Russian term for parapsychology.

PSYCHOGRAPH—the script received by such instruments as the ouija board. A form of ouija board.

PSYCHOGRAPHY—a term used by mediums to denote all forms of spiritual writing.

PSYCHOKINESIS or PK—the ability to move small or large objects with the mind, using the vibrations of the object itself.

PSYCHOLIGICAL BARRIERS—inner energy walls or barriers set up spiritually to protect inner subjective beliefs and thoughts from drifting, and being lost temporarily from ones vision and mind.

PSYCHOLOGICAL EXTENSION—an actual projection of characteristics and psychic energies on the part of the sender and receiver when in a mediumistic trance for the purpose of communication.

PSYCHOLOGICAL WARP—an open channel between a receiver and a sender creating a pathway between physical and spiritual personalities.

PSYCHOLOGY—the science of the psyche or soul. Studying the actions and the reactions of the psyche and physical body.

PSYCHOMANTEUM—ancient Greek oracles of the dead where seekers were able to invoke spirits by gazing into a pool or a pan of water.

PSYCHOMETRIC OBJECT—an object used as a focal point in psychometry.

PSYCHOMETRIST—one who can receive facts concerning an object or its owner by personal contact with the object by listening to it's vibration.

PSYCHOMETRY—the psychic study of receiving facts from an object, about the object or it's owners. A form of divination.

PSYCHON THEORY OF THE MIND—a theory by Carington in which the mind is believed to consist only of psychons (images and data) grouped by means of associative links. He applies the theory to survival, stating that what survives are the psychon systems resulting from previous experiences linked together with other telepathic minds.

PSYCHOPHONE—a term used for all direct psychic communications.

PSYCHOPLASMA—see ectoplasma.

PSYCHOPOMP—a Shaman who helps souls or spirits enter into the next level of existence.

PSYCHORRHAGIC DIATHESIS—psychically sending out a part of one's personality and causing it to appear as a physical object. see apparitions.

PSCHOSOMATIC—a false belief of the psyche. i.e. a person allergic to flowers will sneeze when seeing plastic flowers.

PSYCHOSYNTHESIS—a branch of psychology which believes that in addition to the conscious self or the "I" of an individual, one also has a path way to the "higher self" which is a reflection of the divine reality. The purpose of life is to participate fully in the evolution along that pathway.

PSYCHOTRONICS—another word for parapsychology formed by Czechoslovakian researchers in 1960 who made the statement "psychotronics are the bionics of man." The study of the interaction of matter, energy and consciousness. See parapsychology

PULPIT—symbol of higher consciousness, a teacher.

PULSATIONS OF CONSCIOUSNESS—a belief, from the Seth collection, that the physical reality is "pulsating" from one reality to another, that this existence is but one of the multidimensional reality's in which one exists. see cosmic metabolism. see Seth.

PUMICE—fine-grained volcanic rock used in negative situations to absorb the negativity.

PUMPKIN—symbol of the impossible becoming possible, as in Cinderella.

PURCEL, JACH—the spiritual entity, Lazaris, was channeled by Jach Pursel.

PURGATORY—a Christian belief of an intermediate state after death for the purpose of purification.

PURGE—the cleansing of the energy channels of one's body to allow energy to flow more freely. Used before the beginning of a ritual.

PYGMALION HYPOTHESIS—survival hypothesis proposed by Eisenbud which states that while seemingly surviving entities may be living in certain restricted seances, they are not surviving portions of the deceased, but are re-creations by the living of certain aspects of the deceased. Once organized, such entities may have varying degrees of autonomy, but they continue to exist only for as long as their life is sustained by the living.

PYRITE—brass-yellow mineral which aids healing by playing games and being a jokester.

PYRMID—believed to be the earth in it's maternal state of being. The triangular shape represents the three-fold principle of creation.

PYRMIDOLOGY—the study of, and belief that the dimensions of the great pyramid hold highly advanced scientific knowledge and prophecies of future events.

PYRAMID POWER—speculation exists that the pyramid may be a kind of lens which is able to focus unknown energy by means of its shape. This lens directs cosmic energy to a point one third from its base. Researchers believe that the shape of the pyramid is its "secret".

PYTHAGORAS—6th century B.C.—a Greek philosopher and mathematician who was among the earliest to hold theories of the reincarnation of souls and the mathematical base of all numbers and musical notes. He developed intricate mystical theories involving the basic qualities of numbers. He taught "numbers are everything."

Q

QI GONG—an ancient Chinese belief which involved chanting, deep loud breathing and energy vibration to heal the body.

QUANTUM LEAP—an abrupt change from one discrete energy to another. Sudden increase or advancement.

QUANTUM MECHANICS—a branch of physics measuring the emission or absorption of energy by molecules, atoms and subatomic particles.

QUARTZ—a pure form of silica that forms many minerals. In it's pure state it forms crystals which are used in many forms of psychic events. Colored quartz is used in the art of color healing. see colored quartz.

QUEEN—symbol of one in ruling or high levels. Superior knowledge of the spiritual realm. High priestess of the Goddess belief.

QUEST—to search for something of great value. A search for god in oneself.

QUESTER—one who seeks ancient spiritual knowledge. see spiritual quest migrations.

QUETZALCOATL—a Mayan belief that this God returned as Cortes and will once again appear to bring them, or their present descendants, into Spiritual and Physical freedom. Sometimes refereed to as the Evening Star.

QUIET MIND—a state of mind where no thought, emotion or feeling is present. A state of mind when one is waiting for spiritual imput.

QUIMBANDA—the black magic aspect of the Macumba beliefs of Brazil. see Macumba.

R

RABBIT—the symbol of fertility and speedy growth.

RACIAL BANK OF PSYCHIC KNOWLEDGE—an inner knowledge of all the lives in which one existed i.e. human, animal or plant. A memory of the lines and races in which one existed. See Akashic records.

RADIESTHESIA—implied physical effect of a distant substance upon a divining apparatus. The study of diagnosing disease or searching for lost objects with the use of a pendulum. see radionics.

RADIONICS—all objects emit their own particular radiations. Dowsing is one way of detecting vibrational energies or radiations. The scientific finding of the little "black box" is a tool which aids in the diagnosis and eventual treatment of an illness, it transmits a consistent signal to a patient at their own vibrational frequency. The study of feeling or knowing where there is an energy field. see radiesthesia. see meditation.

RAELIAN MOVEMENT—founded by Claude Vorihon (Rael) in 1973, an ex-car racer. A belief on flying saucers which has an initiation ritual of having a mortician cut out a piece of bone of the third eye which Rael then sends to the extraterrestrials.

RAIN—many meanings. A sadness. A darkening.(as in it's raining on one's life) Spiritual fertilization of life. Spiritual influences upon all mankind. New beginnings of growth.

RAINBOW—many meanings. Believed to be a sign of God for future generations. Love and protection. Colors of the chakras.

RAINBOW BODY— Tibetan Masters are known to have shown themselves in the energy form which is the Rainbow Body. The Chakra colors are that of the rainbow.

RAJA YOGA—speaking to the deity according to Eastern Belief.

RAJA LORD—a Sanskrit word for King. The advanced spirit who has the controlling intelligence of a plane. see King.

RALSTONITE—white colored minerals which promote super-human strength.

RAM'S HEAD—a symbol of war, leadership and power. Aries the ram.

RAMTHA—the spirit entity channeled through the spiritualist J.Z.Knight, who's basic teachings center upon the individuals divine nature.

RAPPING—knocking noises attributed to spirits trying to make contact.

RAPPORT—having compatible communications between the seeker and the seer, good energy exchange between two persons.

RAPS—percussive sounds of varying intensity without visible cause, many such incidents have been recorded throughout history.

RASPITE—yellow to brown colored minerals which assist in the temporary relief of distressing events.

RAT—symbol of hell or death, associated with all plagues.

RAVEN—messenger of the dead. Teachers of magic. Among some Native Americans, Siberians and the Inuit, the Raven was an important God married to the Great Goddess.

RAY—light force. Believed to be seven rays, each to be embodied in great spiritual entities who have specific functions. Some divide the Rays into two groups, Rays of Aspect and Rays of Attribute. see individual ray numbers and groups.

RAYS OF ASPECT—three Rays. The first is the ray of will and power, the second is the ray of love and wisdom, the third is the ray of activity and adaptability. see ray.

RAYS OF ATTRIBUTE—four Rays. The ray of harmony, art, beauty and unity, the ray of science and knowledge, the ray of abstract idealism and devotion and the ray of ceremonial magic and law. see ray.

REACTIVITY—the automatic, spiritually programmed reactions required for self-preservation against harmful actions.

READING—a session with a person perceptive to spiritual energy who has contact with spiritual guides. The spiritual guides use this person as a channel who will then answer all one's questions. Readers use many different forms of media.

REAL ENVIRONMENT—one's spirit which is without space, time, or words. Instant communications. That from where the physical world is formed. The place where the Deity exists.

REAL TIME—normal time in this physical reality. Normal speaking time.

REALITY—in contrast to the illusory, that which actually exists. That which one creates for oneself.

REBIRTH—many meanings. A term meaning reincarnation. A new beginning usually at the choice of the person being born again. A desire to change one's direction of life. To change one's outlook on life. See rebirthing

REBIRTHING—Leonard Orr's technique to transform

the birth trauma into a pleasurable experience. The goal is to achieve breath release the moment one takes one's first breath, thereby breaking the power of the birth trauma of the mind and body. One is submerged into a tub of warm water in the presence of a trained rebirther who goes through the experience with one. see rebirth.

RECEPTIVE ENERGY—that energy which is brought towards oneself as in meditation, calmness or quietness. see projective energy.

RECEIVING CRYSTAL—see left sided crystal.

RECIPROCAL HALLUCINATION—visions or events which are shared by two or more persons in different locations or at great distances apart.

RECORD KEEPER CRYSTAL--recognized by raised triangles on one or more of the triangles faces.

RED LIGHT—(energy) color of the root or base charka. Color used to heal the area of the pelvis and hips. First color of the rainbow. Strongest color used to bring objects toward oneself in the practice of telekinesis.

RED MOON—August 21-September 20. Given this name because of the mist and haze which occur in this month. Thought to be the relaxing month of the deity.

REDDINGITE— a wide range of colored minerals used to assist in the correction of incorrect events.

REEFS—symbol of blockage to destiny, as in the story of Circle in the Odyssey.

REFLEX HEALING—a method of healing by stimulating the autonomous reflex pathways, generally using thumb pressure or massage.

REFLEX MASSAGE—a gliding, smooth use of thumb

pressure used in reflexology.

REFLEXOLOGY—reflex healing through the use of selected points throughout the body. i.e. foot or hand.

REGENERATION—a self healing or transformation through meditation and requesting the Deity for continual energy flow throughout one's being.

REGRESSION—going back in time with the aid of meditation or hypnosis. A form of reliving a past life or lives.

REGRESSION THERAPY—re-experiencing and understanding situations which were traumatic in one's life and/or resulted in forming psychological problems requiring a healing or catharsis.

REIKI—an Oriental belief of balancing the physical energies by brushing the spiritual aura of the physical body.

REINCARNATION—a belief that the soul returns many times to the physical body to learn lessons, help other physical bodies fulfill their journey's or to enter a physical body to be a teacher or mentor. Various lives growing out of the inner self.

REINCARNATION PATTERNS—similar types of incarnation processes.

REINCARNATIONAL CYCLE—the planned and total lives necessary to complete a universal experience.

REINS—symbol of the chakra's joining the physical to the spiritual. Willpower.

RELAXATION—a state of deep rest in which the body slows, the heartbeat slows, the brain waves slow and the blood pressure drops. A state necessary to develop meditation and spiritual growth.

RELEASING—the study of finding a bothersome situation and examining it, accepting it, knowing it cannot be changed and releasing it. A form of healing.

RELIGION—a region or world-view of a way of living. Including a belief in a supreme being, a sense of responsibility before this supreme being, a moral code that must be obeyed, and ritual acts to be performed. Man made belief system which serves a specific God or Deity. Many religions are place and law specific.

RELIGIOUS—following the beliefs of a religion.

REMOTE SENSING—the psychic art which involves psychic impressions of smell, touch, sound and taste at a distance. Astral travelling.

REMOTE VIEWING—seeing people or objects at a distance clairvoyantly with the inner or third eye.

RENAISSANCE—a new beginning or revival.

RENEGADES—warring extra-terrestrial beings who were outlawed and exiled from their home planet after losing a war which they instigated.

REPENTANCE—a change of feelings, mind and purpose in all that relates to the supreme being.

REPLICATION—the duplication of tests by investigators to ensure its findings.

REPRESSING—the art of putting thoughts, disturbing images or feelings out of ones mind and immediate memory.

RESONANCE—the spiritual sensing that something is true.

RESCUE CIRCLE—see rescue work.

RESCUE WORK—the art of freeing lost or "stuck" souls where the physical body has died and the soul still remains on this plane because of a physical desire.

RESPONSIBLE—that which a Medium or Psychic must be when working with people in the spirit realm so as not to frighten or harm them.

REST MOON—November 21-December 20. Given this name because this was the month to rest and communicate with spirit or the Deity. The month of giving thanks for the harvest.

RETENTION— continuity throughout lives. That which one takes from previous lives. i.e. talents and appearances.

RETONE—a form of chanting to realign and retune the energy centers called chakras .see chakras.

RETREAT—a place where one goes to reflect upon oneself. Meditation. To withdraw and grow spiritually.

RETROCOGNITION—sensing or knowing one's past, either this existing life or past lives which could not have been learned by normal means.

RETROGRADE—in Astrology, the planetary condition characterized by an apparent backward motion through the sky. See direct

RETUNE—a form of spiritual chanting or singing used to adjust or realign the energy and energy flow of the chakras. see chakra.

REVERIE—a state of mind that while one is aware of surrounding conditions, the feeling of serenity is so great that the physical reality has no importance. One receives spiritual answers while in this state of mind.

REVIVALS—outbreaks of spiritual mass enthusiasm inspired by mass excitement or persecution.

REVOLT OF THE SLAVES—Atlantean slaves and mutants who revolted in 28,000 B.C. which was a great factor in the sinking of Atlantis.

RHABDIC FORCE—the force which causes muscular contortions in the hands of sensitives. Bending of a hazel switch which is used as a divining rod or oscillating of a pendulum.

RHABDOMANCY—water-witching, divining, dowsing and an art of throwing sticks on the ground to interpret the plans of nature.

RHODONITE—a variety of colored minerals with black veins, used to balance the yin-yang energies.

RICKARDITE—deep-purple crystal which assists in the creation or earning of money.

RIGHT—that which agrees with one's moral standards, spiritual and physical acts. see wrong.

RIGHT HAND PATH— the path of positively and goodness, the path of spiritual evolution and growth. see left hand path.

RIGHT IDENTIFICATION— knowing and understanding oneself as a timeless infinite spiritual light entity.

RIGHT IMAGINATION—to think and manifest that which is required by one for growth. Believing one creates one's own reality.

RING—symbol of the eternally repeated cycle of time and existence. Ancient and traditional symbol of the joining of two, to create one as in marriage. Spiritual-physical joining. Three rings represent the Triple Goddess.

RING-PASS-NOT—a energy ring which surrounds the earth to protect persons from entering areas outside the ring, for which they are not yet prepared spiritually and that which is beyond their powers.

RIPENING—a spiritual practice where a person advances slowly or "ripens" then realizes that s\he has reached their goal.

RISHI—a saint, seer or medium.

RITUAL—a repetition of movements or actions to set a "groove" in the universe, thus receiving greater energy every time these actions or movements are repeated. The practice of set procedures. Ceremony.

RIVER—a symbol of continuation and immortality. A creative power of time and nature.

ROBERTS, JANE—(1929-1984) best known for the channelling of the entity called Seth.

ROD OF SOLOMON—a "Y-Rod" used for dowsing prepared in accordance with elaborate Caballistic Rite. see Y-Rod. see Caballistic Rite

ROGUE PLANET—a planet forced out of orbit by warfare causing it to collide with other celestial bodies. This has a great impact on spiritual energies.

ROLPHING—a deep massage program which softens chronically tight connective tissue, allowing the skeleton to ride easily, thus making the whole body feel lighter. Ida Rolph's Technique

ROOT ASSUMPTION—the built in ideas of reality. i.e. the sun rises, one must eat and drink to survive, it is dark at night, etc.

ROOT CHAKRA—the energy point at the base of the spine, color-red, stone-jasper, tone-do.

ROOT RACE—one of the seven races of humankind which evolve upon a planet, believed to be necessary to complete a cycle of planetary existence, called a world period. see individual root race numbers.

ROSARY—a string of beads used as a focal point of prayer in the Christian Belief.

ROSCHERITE—green-brown mineral used to provide a comfortable, safe and loving home-life.

ROSE—represents love, beauty, passion and desire. The flower of Venus.

ROSE QUARTZ—rose colored crystal used to enhance the presentation of the self. The sensual self.

ROSICRUCIANS—founded in the fifteenth century by Christian Rosenkreutz, whose name translates to Rosy Cross. The order of the Rosy Cross or Roscrucianism claims to be the oldest secret society in the Western World dating back to the ancient Egyptain mystery schools. Beliefs include, reincarnation, psychic healings and the White Brotherhood.

ROTATION—clockwise rotations create positive or highly creative energies; counter-clockwise rotations create negative or destructive energies.

ROUND TABLE—symbol of universal or spiritual realms. The twelve knights symbolized the twelve signs of the Zodiac.

RUBY—a variety of colors, the most common ruby-red. Colored crystals are used to encourage stability in all areas of one's life.

RUTILATED QUARTZ CRYSTALS—a crystal with line-type markings within itself.

RULER—Each sign of the Zodiac is said to have a ruler or ruling planet. When one is born with the sun in any given sign of the zodiac, it may then be said that that one is to be ruled by the planet which rules that sign.

RULERSHIP—in Astrology, a strong connection between a planet and a sign, allowing a clear expression of both.

RUN—a series of trials in an ESP or PK test, A run of 25 trials is most often used in ESP testing and 24 dice throws in PK tests.

RUNES—ancient Egyptian Stones. Used for healing. An aid for foreseeing the future, although never giving direction, but leaving one to practice the freedom of choice. The true meaning was lost with the Ancients when the Runestones were lost for four hundred years, last used in Iceland in the middle ages. see petra.

S

SABBAT—an assembly of witches and wizards which is held every three months.
SACRED PIPE—sacred to Native Americans, tobacco smoke is equivalent to visible breath or incense. Used in rituals.
SACREAL CHAKRA—the eighth chakra in the Hindu belief, other beliefs have seven chakras.
SACRIFICE—the offering or giving up of something pleasing to the Deity.
SAGITTARIUS—the Zodiac sign,"the archer" November 22-December 21.
SAI BABA—(1926-?) Hindu avatar who is renowned for his teachings and healings.
SAINT—a holy person in the Christian Belief.
SAINT ELMO'S FIRE—named after Saint Erasmus. A natural very high voltage effect seen on the mast of a sailing ship warning of a coming storm.
SAINT GERMAIN—an ascended master considered to be the greatest adept since Jesus Christ. Believed to have had many lives on this earth as a great teacher. see adept.
SALAMANDER—a symbol of one that is able to live in the midst of adversity or fire. Strength to continue.
SALEM WITCH TRIALS—began in 1692 in Salem Massachusetts and stopped when the wife of Governor Phipps was accused of being a witch. Marked in history books to be one of the most disgraceful episodes in the History of America.
SALIENCE EFFECT—a telepathy test where a tendency for hits or correct guesses arise at a particular position on the score sheet.
SANDSTONE—a com-

pressed sand which provides insight into deceit.

SANGOMA—an African Spiritual healer who uses the energies or powers of Ancient ancestors.

SANSKRIT—an ancient language given by the great Aryian, Panini. Believed to be used in some Buddhist Churches. Some believe it to be the classical language of the Brahmans known as a "mystery language". Never known or spoken in its systematized form except by superior Brahmans.

SANTERIA—Afro-Cuban belief in which African Dieties are worshipped.

SAPPHIRE—a mineral with a wide range of colors. The common blue star sapphire is a "stone of wisdom."

SAT—a Sanskrit word which means truth.

SATAN—the Christian, Old Testament personality who gave the personification of evil to many stories. The Devil.

SATANISM—the worship of Satan and other negative forces.

SATURNIZATION—in Astrology, an introspect formed by one's Saturn to any point on another's birthchart, symbolizing the crystallization and confrontation, or frustration and control of the affected point.

SCALES—justice. Cause and effect. Good balance. A sign that all is as it should be.

SCARAB BEETLE—an ancient Egyptain belief that the beetle was a form of sun God, carved of jade, limestone or stone and usually buried with a deceased person. Placed where the heart is located, the heart is taken out of the body when one is embalmed.

SCEPTOR—a symbol of the thunderbolt. Thor's hammer. The phallus and the magic wand.

SCEPTRE CRYSTAL—a natural formed crystal with the base being penetrated by a crystal rod.

SCIENCE OF CREATIVE INTELLIGENCE—a detailed study of the process that determines the way the mind works. A systematic knowledge (science) about the changes in the energy of the universe leading directly to creativity in relation to a consciousness of the abstract, such as energy and happiness.

SCHLIEREN PHOTOGRAPHY—a form of photography which measures the air flows and disturbances, heat waves and odic energy waves. see Kirlian photography.

SCIENTOLOGY—the religion that has its base in dianetics. see dianetics.

SCORPIO—the Zodiac sign, "the scorpion". October 23-November 21.

SCRIBES—a person who made scripts in the days before printing was invented. Printers of old.

SCRIPTURES—books of the Christian Bible. Old writings.

SCROLLS—that upon which was written the Divine Law or hidden mysteries.

SCRYING—the use of a crystal as a means of seeing the future. A focal point for predictions of events. Crystal-gazing. see speculum.

SCYTHE—the shape is symbolic of the moon. Instrument of the Grim Reaper.

SEAL OF SOLOMON—two interlocking triangles symbolizing the merging of the duality's. Male/female. Conscious/subconscious. Day/night. Downward pointing triangle represents the negative energy, and the upward pointing triangle represents the positive energy.

SEAMANITE—small yellow needle-like crystals which stimulates the desire to create.

SEANCE— a gathering of people with like thinking to make contact with the spirit world lead by a sensitive.

SEAX-WICCA—differs from Gardnerian Witchcraft by following a Saxon background and allowing self-initiation. It is organized so that every coven elects its presiding priests and priestess annually and democratically.

SECOND SIGHT—supernatural perception at a distance of time and space. Seeing and hearing complete scenes and conversations at a distance. Extrasensory awareness of objects. The power to perceive objects not normal to the physical senses. see clairvoyance.

SECOND RAY—the ray of love and wisdom. Young lover's ray. see Ray.

SECOND ROOT RACE—members of a people held by the Ancient Greeks to live beyond the North Wind in a region of perpetual sunshine. The ancient Arctic Peoples.

SECONDARY CONSTRUCTIONS—a pseuo-form of oneself projected without one's knowledge when one is deep in thought, with emotion and feelings about an event or person. Often seen in the astral planes. See pseudo-form.

SECONDARY PERSONALITY—an additional or extra subordinate personality resulting from dissociation.

SECRETS OF THE UNIVERSE—knowledge given to Spiritual Warriors concerning the mechanics and networking of the Universe. see Spiritual Warrior.

SEDONA, ARIZONA, USA—said to be one of the powerful psychic energy points of the world.

SEEKER—one who desires to receive information or direction from paranormal sources, generally through a medium or psychic.

SEER—one who is sensitive to psychic energy. Clairvoyant. One who is able to foretell the future. A medium.

SEFIRAH—the ten stages of God's revelation in the Kabalah.

SELF-FULFILLING PROPHECY—the process by which one's desires and expectations are fulfilled through one's own beliefs and behaviour. Being unaware of the connection of belief, behaviour and fulfillment.

SELF-HEALED CRYSTAL—a crystal which has been broken off of its growing base and has re-grown small crystal-like crystals at it's base. The beginning of a new crystal group.

SELF-HYPNOSIS—putting oneself in a sleep-like state for the purpose of learning, healing or making contact with others.

SELF-SUSTAINING PRINCIPLE—having the belief that one creates one's own reality and that one creates that which is necessary for self-sustainment such as fruit trees, water, gardens and fibre for clothing.

SENSA—the secret language or mystery speech of the initiated Adepts throughout the planet. It is mainly a hieroglyphic cipher.

SENSITIVE—a psychic. One who has the ability to see, feel or hear from the spiritual realm or other side. The ability to make contact with the spirit world.

SENSORY AUTOMATISM—visual or auditory imagery. Sometimes fully externalized without ones conscious direction.

SENTIENT—a form of sensing, feeling, hearing or knowing without learning. Spiritual contact. Gut feeling. Intuition.

SENZAR—a mystery language used by adepts. see sensa.

SEPTEMBER MOON—known as the Harvest Moon. The month that all things planted, and naturally grown, were harvested. see Harvest Moon.

SERAPIS—a healing Egyptain divinity. The Serapeum at Alexandria was one of the seven wonders of the world.

SERIALITY—an assumed universal principle that operates without physical intervention that brings similar events together. A natural physical or spiritual gathering.

SERPENT—many meanings. A symbol of Deceit. Secrecy. Subtlety. Wisdom. The serpent tempts one to look inside and gain self-knowledge. The Kundalini. Intertwined serpents around a staff represent healing.

SERPANT BITING IT'S TAIL—represents the law of endless learning, growth and transformation.

SERPENT WOMAN—Aztec belief of a Deity who presided over the designated chores of feeding and attending to the needs of the Gods.

SERPENTINE—fibrous-like green to brown mineral which helps in the rise of the kundalini. see kundalini.

SEVEN—the number of the mysteries and the mystic. Relates to the soul development and completion of the reincarnation process to this planet. Wisdom. Perfection.

SEVENTH RAY—the ray of spiritual energy and spiritual law. see Ray.

SETH—an entity channeled through Jane Roberts (Butts).

SEX CHOICE—many beliefs. Sex choices can be chosen arbitrarily. Male or female is chosen according to the required life experience. One's sex choice may come about by accident.

SEX DETERMINATION—a dowsing practice used mainly in eggs. A circular swing of the pendulum signifies a female bird and a backward and forward swing signifies a male bird.

SEXTILE— Astrology, an aspect characterized by a 60-degree separation between two planets, symbolizing the process of excitation.

SHADOW—an Ancient belief that this was the part of the soul that went to the underworld.

SHAKERS—an 18th century religious cult. An offshoot of the Quakers which believed in celibacy. This cult was appealing to some women so it became a type of feminist movement, it was short lived.

SHAMAN—originated in the Asian Arctic, one who healed by contacting the spirits. A Medicine Man. A Witch Doctor. A Healer.

SHAMBALAH—(Shamballa) many meanings. The planetary center founded by the Ancient Atlanteans who now guide the race of humankind. The city of the Gods which is in the West to some cultures, in the East to other cultures and in the North or South to still others. A sacred island in the Gobi Dessert. The home of secret doctrine and mysticism. A mystical city in Oriental Folklore, apx. 1600 B.C.

SHAPE-SHIFTING—changing the shape or shifting the physical body.

SHEEP—a term for one who believes in ESP.

SHEEP\GOAT HYPOTHESIS—a hypothesis which states that if one believes in ESP or the paranormal (sheep), when one is tested s\he will score higher than one who disbelieves in ESP or the paranormal (goat).

SHELL—symbol of the Mother Goddess.

SHELLFISH—represents the early stages of conscious growth or unfoldment. A wakening of the consciousness.

SHE'OL—another term for hell or Hades.

SHIATSU—a Japanese stylized method of massaging the tsubos, either through applying pressure with the fingers and hands, or through the use of elbows, knees and feet. There are many forms of Shiatsu. Combined with Acupuncture in some cases. See tsubos.

SHIELD—a spiritual cocoon type of energy surrounding one for protection of psychic attack.

SHINTO— a Japanese belief system of Ancestor Worship, links living Japanese to their ancestral spirit.

SHIP—a journey through life in a physical sense. Representing present or future physical treasure.

SHIUR QOMAH—a controversial fifth century mystical text describing the figure that was enthroned on the spiritual chariot of the Christian Bible. see throne mysticism.

SHOWER MOON—April 19-May 19. Given this name because of the many warming showers in this month. see moons

SHROUD OF TURIN—a yellow strip of linen, blood stained and bearing the image of a bearded man. Found in a French church in 1353 believed to be the shroud in which Jesus was buried. Fourteen feet in length and four feet in width.

SHUT DOWN—the state of one's spiritual condition when one believes they can no longer carry on in the spiritual realm. A spiritual event making one feel they no longer have the spiritual right, consciously or unconsciously, harming or healing another. see silent

SIBYL—a female divine. A prophetess.

SIDDHIS—Patanjali's Book 3 refers to the Siddhis as highly trained masters with unbelievable spiritual powers.

SIDEREAL ASTROLOGY—a form of astrology which takes into consideration the precision of the earth's axis. see tropical astrology.

SIDEREAL TIME—an astronomically exact time used in setting up birthcharts.

SIGN—an paranormal indication of an event. In Astrology, one of the twelve basic divisions of the zodiac. A phase in the orbital relationship of the earth and the sun. A fundamental psychological process.

SIGNIFICATOR—in Astrology each planet stands for or symbolizes certain things and qualities. i.e. Venus is the signifacator of beauty and harmony.

SILENT—a state of mind when a Psychic feels that s\he has lost their psychic or spiritual powers. see shut down.

SILVA MIND CONTROL—a paranormal system developed by Jose Silva which develops improved memory, learning ability and all paranormal powers.

SILVER—metal of the moon, female energy. Mineral to assist a person who lives alone. It brings one all the advantages of life.

six

SILVER CORD—a Metaphysical belief of a lifeline which connects the physical body and its higher bodies or spirit. This spiritual lifeline breaks at death.
SIMPLE—a state in which to keep all psychic and spiritual teachings, events, learning and practices, as opposed to intellectualization.
SIMPLE EXISTANCE—a style of living that includes all forms of pleasure, work, song and dance. Lived without effort. Enjoying the moment.
SIMPLE CONSCIOUSNESS—it is believed that each atom or molecule has its own consciousness, that this consciousness always stays with the body even when the consciousness or soul leaves , as in the sleep state. The individual atom consciousness is then called the simple consciousness or body overseer. see body consciousness.
SIMPLE OUT OF BODY EXPERIENCE— when the psychic or etheric body departs from the physical body as opposed to all of the soul leaving.
SINGLETON—any planet or world, placed or existing alone in the hemispheres.
SINGULARIZATION—an existing personality splitting off another personality. A sub personality.
SITTER—one who asks a medium for a psychic reading. Requesting information about the future.
SITTING—many meanings. Receiving a reading. Joining in a seance or listening to evolved spiritual persons. Part of an ESP experiment consisting of all the trials made at one session.
SIX—balance and fair treatment. A solid number represented by the double single inverted triangles or the seal

of Solomon. Female energies. A solid number of the mind.

SIXTH RAY—the ray of Spiritual Idealism and Devotion. see ray.

SIXTH SENSE—the source and sum of all our senses. The psychic sense. The spirit.

SKELETON—remains of the physical body. Symbol of death and destruction.

SKEPTIC—one who is not sure of his beliefs or if one believes another's beliefs.

SKIN VISION—the ability of one to see by touching. Seeing through feeling or touching.

SKOTOGRAPH—spirit writing or painting on a wide variety of topics. Voices and writings on newly purchased, unopened audio cassettes and writing paper.

SKY GOD—the supreme Deity known by many cultures as the Sole God or creator of the planet Earth. see high God.

SKY WOMAN— Iroquois belief of a Goddess Woman who travels through all space and who created the planet Earth.

SLATE WRITING—the paranormal appearance of written messages on a slate in the presence of a medium.

SLEEP—a state of unconsciousness in which the body is being replenished with energy from an unseen world. Many cultures associate sleep with death.

SMELLS—scents from the psychic world. see perfumes.

SMOKE—believed to ward off or cleanse negative energies. A cleansing ritual. see smudging.

SMOKEY QUARTZ—gray to black quartz crystals used to help refine the energies when one is in meditation.

SMUDGING—a ceremony using smoke to purify the

physical body in preparation for rituals. see smudgestick and smoke.

SMUDGESTICK—a stick wrapped in sage, cedar, or mugwort used in smudging. see smudging.

SNOW-MOON—February 20-March 20, named after the beauty of the white snow which is abundant in this month. Related to pure spirit. see moons.

SOAPSTONE—multi-colored white soft stone which enhances truthfulness in emotions and feelings.

SOLAR CROSS—a cross with all four arms being equal in length representing the union of the female -horizontal, negative energy and the male -vertical, positive energy.

SOLARIZATION—in Astronomy, an intraspect made by one's sun to any point on another's chart, symbolizing the process of revitalization or domination of the affected point.

SOLAR PLEXUS—the nerve mass behind the stomach which services most of the involuntary organs. One of the Chakra points.

SOLAR PLEXUS CHAKRA—energy point located in the center of the abdomen, believed by the Ancients to be the center of the soul. Color-yellow or gold, stone-citrine, tone-me, gland-pancreas

SOLIPSISM—the theory that nothing but the self exists.

SOLSTICE—the day of the year when the night is longest (winter solstice) and the day of the year when the day is longest (summer solstice).

SOMNAMBULISM—sleep walking. A state of a half-waking trance where one is suddenly highly intelligent, believed to be that of psychic or universal intelligence.

SONOPUNCTURE—ultrasound therapy at an acupuncture point. The ultrasound is usually directed through the use of a vibrating quartz crystal on a layer of mineral oil.

SONOLITE—red, orange and brown minerals used to enhance the masculine aspects of the personality.

SOOTHSAYER—one who foretells the future. A medium. A diviner.

SORCERER—one who has the use of power gained from the control of evil spirits. Wizard.

SORCERY—a magic used to evil ends. Black magic.

SORTILEGE—a variety of divination means. Such as dice, bones, stones, sticks or other objects cast upon the ground and the pattern then being read.

SOUL—the non-material immortal part of a person. The spiritual part of a person. The God part of a physical body. That which one is. The continually reincarnating entity. The Ancients believed there was but one soul which connected all creation.

SOUL CHOICE TIME—a time in between incarnations when the spirit or soul looks back on the just completed lifetime and decides what and where the next incarnation will be.

SOUL MATE—many meanings. This term became very popular in the Western World apx. 1970. Not often heard in the Eastern beliefs. A soul's ideal counterpart. A soul's helper in this existence. Necessary for true happiness. Having good spiritual relationships.

SOUL PERSONALITY—that which is the self. The perfect essence in man. The personality which man must gradually evolve and return to the godhead..

SOUNDS—unknown sounds or noises heard in seances or spiritual gatherings, believed to be from the psychic world.

SOURCE—the spirit within which responds when called upon.

SOURCE-MAN'S— the abstract or principle of one's being. That which allows growth and change.

SPACE—that area between the objects one perceives and oneself. The place where time comes into existence.

SPACELORDS—extra-terrestrials who settled in Atlantis, then intermarried with humans to help in their physical and spiritual advancement.

SPEAKING IN TONGUES—speech usually not understood, believed to be divinely inspired. A form of automatism. The physical person being used by spirit to deliver a message. see glossolalia.

SPECTRAL FLAMES—supernatural lights seen in cemeteries, around churches and on open land. see luminous phenomenon.

SPECULARII—a 16th century name for crystal gazers.

SPECULUM—any mirror, crystal, metal surface or shiny object which can be used for scrying. see scrying.

SPELL—a magical ritual usually accompanied by spoken words directed towards another person or object. A reaction to a state of mind imposed on a person by another person who has the ability to plant a verbal seed and make it grow. Can be either positive or negative.

SPHALERITE—a mineral with a variety of colors, used to balance both male and female aspects of one's personality.

SPHERE—divisions of the spirit world, both in a spatial

and spiritual sense. A spiritual dimension. An orb. The earth.

SPHINX—the symbol of the combination of the animal and human attributes.

SPIDER—many meanings. Creation. Existence. The Pueblo myth tells of a Spider Woman who spun the universe into creation, The Kiowa belief is similar except it was a Spider Grandmother who spun the Universe into Creation.

SPINEL—crystals in the form of pebbles, cubes and octahedral shapes used to help renew energy, keeps energy flowing.

SPIRIT—an invisible entity. An entity without a physical body. It's opposite is Matter.

SPIRIT BODY—another name for soul. The ever-living portion of the physical body. That which creates the physical reality.

SPIRIT CHILDREN—children who have passed over or died and are growing to maturity on the spirit side of reality, usually accidental deaths.

SPIRIT GUIDE—a spiritual entity who chooses to remain close to a person for the purpose of guidance. Guardian Angel.

SPIRIT HYPOTHESIS—the theory that one's consciousness survives death and may be communicated with by living persons. The theory that the intelligence which directs a medium is a disembodied spirit.

SPIRIT INTERVENTION—unrequested spiritual assistance in finding lost articles.

SPIRIT PHOTOGRAPHY—first came to be in 1861 when William Mumler took a picture of himself and the image of a dead person appeared in the picture. Many images have been reported since then.

SPIRIT REALM—the planes surrounding and interpenetrating the earth where spiritual entities dwell.

SPIRITISM—the more accurate and appropriate term for spiritualism. see spiritualism.

SPIRITOID—a term for messages which originate in the subconscious mind and appear in a dramatic form.

SPIRITUALISM—a belief that the spirits of those passed over, or dead, survive and can communicate with the living by mediumistic communications or tapping. A belief on life after death.

SPIRITUAL—a practice of goodness and unconditional love. Doing good unto others. A belief on the deity, god or the universe. Obeying the messages of the deity or universe. The practice of working very hard to become a better person in all areas of ones life.

SPIRITUAL EMERGENCE—the sudden arrival at new levels, or dimensions of spiritual growth without effort.

SPIRITUAL HEALING—the art of one becoming a channel for energy from the Deity, which passes through one and is directed at another requiring healing. One may also channel deity energy without the energy passing through oneself, instead directing it directly to the one requiring a healing.

SPIRITUAL LAW—natural law. Any networking truth which operates upon the earth as law, i.e. born to die, love brings love, hate brings hate.

SPIRITUAL QUEST MIGRATIONS—three large groups of Atlanteans who left Atlantis, after the revolt of the slaves, in search of spiritual knowledge. Most of whom settled in Egypt and Western Europe. see revolt of the slaves.

SPIRITUAL SEANCES—a group of people gathered together to communicate with spirits or to watch spiritual phenomenon. Another term for seance. see seance.

SPIRITUALISM—a spiritual way of life. A belief that all is connected through one soul or spirit.

SPIRITUALIST—one who believes in the ability of mediums to contact the spirits of the dead. One who believes in spiritualism.

SPIRITUAL CHANNEL—an invisible spiritual channel of energy running from the top of the head to the base of the torso. The seven main chakras lie on the spiritual channel. see chakra and energy.

SPIRITUAL LEAVE OF ABSENCE—a time for one to remain free of all Spiritual events. A time necessary to clear the mind and reflect on one's own Spiritual position.

SPIRITUAL PERCEPTION—looking at a situation from a spiritual standpoint rather than a physical one. Seeing beyond the physical normal reality.

SPIRITUAL REGENERATION MOVEMENT—an organization designed to teach Transcendental Meditation and its spiritual lifestyle.

SPIRITUAL WARRIOR—one who has been given the gift and power to control the elements such as wind, rain and teleportation. A Spiritual person who has devoted most of his\her life to Spirituality.

SPIRULINA—a highly nutritious form of plankton used by the Japanese for health problems, it is believed to be the answer for the worlds food shortage. Believed to be a form of "manna" that the Hebrews ate in the desert in the Christian Bible.

SPONTANEOUS PSI EXPERIENCE—natural unplanned occurrence of an event or experience which appears to involve parapsychical ability or spiritual intervention.

SPRITES—a spiritual entity commonly called a fairy or elf.

SQUARE—in Astrology, an aspect characterized by a separation of ninety degrees between two planets, symbolizing the process of friction..

SRI—a form of address. i.e. sir, mr., esq, etc..

STAFF—symbol of a helper. Extra power. Spirit guide.

STAG—a symbol similar to the Tree of Life because of it's branching antlers.

STANNITE—metallic to steel-gray colored grain-type crystals used to widen the pathway of personal power enhancement, both physical and spiritual.

STAR—a celestial body appearing as a luminous point in the night sky. A beacon to guide one on the journey through the subconscious. Used in the study of Astrology.

STARCHILD—one who has experienced many incarnations whose main purpose is to service humankind. Very brilliant in ones young years.

STARCLAD—a ritual of Wicca in which one is nude.

STARHAWK—one of the best known current leaders of the Neo-Pagan movements who provided the movement with a theory of political action. Starhawk is a student of Wicca.

STAR LIGHT ESSENCES—a vibrational preparation made by focusing the light of stars into pure water. Used as floral essences.

STATE OF BECOMING—necessary experiences or lives on one's journey back to the godhead or beginning. Reality is always in a state of becoming.

STATE OF CONSCIOUSNESS—any distinct or altered state of awareness including dreamstate, hypnotic state, alpha state or normal beta state.

STATION—in astrological terms a planet is said to be making a station when it is stationary or without movement.

STATIONARY—an Astrological term meaning a planet is stationary when it appears to be standing motionless relative to the zodiac, about to turn retrograde or direct.

STATIONARY DIRECT—in astrological terms, a planet which is stationary and then turns direct.

STATIONARY RETROGRADE—in astrological terms, a planet which is stationary and then turns retrograde.

STELLIUM—in Astrology, any cluster of three or more planets in a single house.

STEPS—entrance or communication between different levels of consciousness.

STIBIOTANTALITE—yellow to brown to red crystals used to block unwanted energies from other worlds. A shield.

STIGMATA—the appearance of marks on the body or skin which correspond to the wounds suffered by Christ during the crucifixion. Birthmarks usually in the form of blotches or marks on the skin. The best known birth stigmata is a skin blotch where the previous incarnation was fatally wounded. Any aid that has memory of a previous life.

STILLNESS—an inner state of mind without mental activity. Preparation for spiritual activity. A state of meditation.

STONE—symbolizes the union of the spirit and the body, the father and the son, the mother and the daughter. The dwelling place of Primordial power. God and goddess power.

STONEHENGE—the most famous ancient megalithic site in the world located in Wiltshire England. The original purpose of the site is unknown. Some of the reported reasons for its existence are: landing place of U.F.O.s; the place of the Druids; place of great psychic power. Built apx.3500 B.C. to 1100 B.C.

STORK—the bearer of new things to come. Good news.

STORM—a symbol of unpleasant experiences of life and their consequences. Creation, causing the joining of the Elements.

STRAWBERRY MOON—June22-July 22, named after the abundance and beauty of strawberries and their aromatic flowers which are naturally produced in this month. see moons.

STREAM—symbolizes the continuum of life.

STRENGITE—violet-red crystals used to strengthen and increase the power of the silver cord. see silver cord.

STRUCTURAL REINTERGRATION—see Rolfing.

STUDENT—one who has a teacher or master from whom s\he is learning the secrets and mysteries of the universe or the deity.

SUBCONSCIOUS—that which knows and sees all.

The "computer" of the physical personal reality. The meeting place of the inner and outer ego. Directly related to the divinity or the universe.

SUBJECTIVE—a conscious inner state having to do with conception, will, recollection, imagination and reason.

SUBJECTIVE DIMENSIONS—a limitless and complete inner record of knowledge of all one's lives, experiences and events which have occurred since the beginning of time.

SUBJECTIVE OPENINGS—see subjective warps.

SUBLIMATION—the redirection of basic energy, especially sexual, into more socially acceptable events or occasions. see celebacy.

SUBLIMINAL—a sound or other stimulus that is too weak to be heard or perceived consciously, but is perceived subconsciously. Some believe that the soul or spirits often communicate on this level.

SUBLIMINAL PERCEPTION—perception beneath the level of conscious awareness.

SUBTLE BODY—another term meaning aura. see aura.

SUBTLE LEVEL OF THOUGHTS—the progression of the mind, from attention to abstract notions and thoughts, is believed to be the highest of consciousness. "Higher", "refined" and "fine" are the levels of thoughts.

SUCCUBUS—a Female Demon choosing to having sex with human males. see Incubus.

SUDDEN EXCESS ENERGY—a sudden large amount of spiritual energy felt in one's body used for the purpose of sending another a spiritual healing, usually a subconscious request from the one who needs it.

SUFI—mystics from the Middle East whose goal is to perfect the human mind and heart so one may transcend ordinary human limitations. see Sufism.

SUFISM—(900 A.D.) a Middle East belief based on Mohammedanism. A branch of Islam that teaches personal mysticism and union with Allah or God. The mystics and mystical spirituality of Islam.

SUGGESTION—a quiet, subtle command from the conscious to the subconscious mind for the use of creating an outer or physical reality.

SULPHUR—a yellow mineral which carries a negative charge used to promote an abundance of energy.

SUMMERLAND—the higher planes of consciousness. The Metaphysical equivalent of the Christian heaven.

SUMMUM BONUM—the supreme or highest good.

SUN—life force. Gold metal. The heart of the Spirit. Power of prime matter.

SUNDANCE—a spiritual ceremony of Native Americans for health, fertility and food. Banned in the USA because of the elements of self-sacrifice, which were considered to be barbaric.

SUNSTONE—a variety of colors, the crystals are used to encourage independence. Called the "luck stone" in gambling.

SUNFLOWER—represents nature at it's fullest, happiness within, peace, serenity.

SUN SIGN—in astrology, the constellation closest to the sun at birth.

SUPERCONSCIOUS—the higher self. The god self. The spiritual portion of the physical reality. God.

SUPERNATURAL—an occurrence in violation of natural law. Any phenomenon for which there is no apparent explanation. (in contrast to the paranormal where science may one day find an explanation.)

SUPERNORMAL—an older term for paranormal or supernatural.

SUPERNORMAL COGNITION—a synonym for ESP.

SUPERSENSE—the sixth sense. The intuitive and psychic awareness.

SUPERSENSONICS—the psychic sensing of subtle variations which emanate from the universe or spirit realm. see sensitive.

SUPERSHEEP—one who has a strong belief on ESP and the paranormal. One who also believes that they possess these abilities. see whitesheep.

SUPERSTITIOUS DEBRIS—beliefs one was taught which clutter one's growth. Physical reality untruths.

SUPRALUMINAL VELOCITY—speed faster than that of light, as in psychic projections which are instantaneous.

SURREALISM—a movement in art that emphasizes the expression of spiritual or subconscious images.

SURRENDER—an attitude of non-reactivity and greatly reduced ego in which the conscious mind accepts what "is" at this moment, and is prepared to be guided by spiritual wisdom into the next moment.

SURVIVAL PACT—a method of providing evidence for the existence of an afterlife. An agreement between two persons that the first one to pass on will attempt to contact the other.

SWALLOW—symbol of returning. Spring. Growth of nature. Sacred to Venus and Isis.

SWAMI— a spiritual teacher of the Eastern belief. A Guru.

SWAN—symbol of a desire turned to reality. Messengers of the Great Goddess. The Valkyries wore swan feather clothing on occasion. see Valkyries.

SWASTIKA—similar to the cross. The solar wheel of the seasons.

SWEAT—a form of spiritual steam bath performed by Native Americans in a specially built lodge. Believed to purify the body and spirit.

SWIFT AND SURE WAY—another term for ladder path. see ladder path.

SWORDS—one of the suits of the Tarot representing activity, either destructive or constructive. Action.

SYLPH—believed to be an element of air, similar to a cupid.

SYMBOL—a mark represent an event, a gathering, a group or an object.

SYMBOLISM—the art of using a symbol to recognize an act, place or event. i.e. dark clouds symbolizing a storm.

SYMBOLOGY—the study of symbols. Reading events by interpreting symbols. Pictures or events that have specific meaning that relate to other specific events.

SYMPATHETIC AFFINITY—the theory that persons or objects which have a similar shape, character or composition have a strong bond or attraction to each other. Like attracts like. Spiritual persons attract spiritual persons.

SYMPATHETIC MAGIC—similar objects which react to magic in a similar fashion.

SYNASTRY—the astrology of human relationships. An astrological counselling session. Foreseeing the future.

SYNCHRONICITY—separate events which seem to have the appearance of being linked, but between which, there is no clear logical connection.

SYSTEM—A complete "whole" involving inter-acting and inter-dependent parts in which a basic law, among these parts, is maintained. A set of rules pertaining to a complete networking. In Astrology, a type of composite chart that resembles one's partner's chart more than the one's own, indicating that the circumstances seem to grant more power to the person whose chart the composite chart resembles. see system artificial and system natural.

SYSTEM (ARTIFICIAL)—non-spiritual or biological systems designed in every detail by human beings such as televisions, computers, cars etc. see system.

SYSTEMS (NATURAL)—spiritual or biological systems not designed by humans such as organs, plants, molecules, atoms and cells. see system.

SYSTEM OF REALITIES—the networking of all realities in all area's of the universe.

T

TABARD—a Sorcerer's ceremonial robe worn during magical ceremonies. It consists of two rectangles sewn together at the top corners and then belted.

TABLE OF HOUSES—an astrological book used on complex calculations in spherical trigonometry that shows the location of house cusps at various times and latitudes.

TABLE TILTING or TAPPING—spiritual means of foreseeing the future with a prearranged signal. i.e. one tap means "yes" and two taps mean "no."

TABOO—a prohibition of any human action or object which would provoke a Deity.

TAI CHI—a Chinese method of self-defense and exercise. Creates good health and spiritual awareness.

TALISMAN—an object similar to an amulet but made for a specific purpose, believed to be endowed with supernatural powers, which transfers this power to its owner. see charge.

TALMUD—the classical Rabbinic discussions of the ancient code of Jewish Law.

TANKA—a Buddhist spiritual painting which stimulates the unconscious and awareness. The name of a Japanese poetic form.

TANTIC YOGA—the art of transforming sensual energy and experience into spiritual energy.

TANTRA—a set of Hindu scriptures used in the worship of "Shakti", the female personification of the Hindu deity. Introduced to the West in 1929.

TANTRISM—an Eastern belief or religion which involves sexual practices.

TANZANITE—blue or purple crystals called the "stones

of magic" which manifest the physical reality almost upon request.

TAOISM—(apx. 600 B.C.) Chinese belief meaning the way, the principle of Truth.

TAPAS—daily training required to become a Yogis

TARGET—the item, object or symbol being guessed in an ESP test. The mineral or object searched for by a dowser

TAROT CARDS— ancient Egyptain Cards used to tell fortunes. Believed to be thousands of years old. Seventy eight cards in a deck..

TAROMANCY—the art of foreseeing the future or divination with the use of Tarot Cards.

TASSILI-N-AJJER— caves in the Sahara Dessert which have paintings, believed to be apx. 8000 years old, which appear to be that of spiritual persons dowsing.

TATTOO—symbol of sacri fice dedicated to the design through the flow of blood.

TAURUS—the Zodiac sign "the bull" April 20-May 20.

TEACHER—one whose occupation is to instruct. Intelligent persons or spirit guides that share their knowledge and experience with their students. A Mormon ranking above a Deacon in the Aaronic priesthood.

TEA LEAF READING— the belief that the patterns formed by tea leaves at the bottom of a cup are indicators of a greater truth. The method used by gypsies. The leaves and the ritual involved differ with each reader.

TEAM UP—some use this directive to mean the joining and believing in, or on, the Deity or Universe.

TEETH—the Ancients believed that one could be marked by spiritual teeth, marks were for both positive or negative reasons.

TEKTITE—meteoritic glass from outer space which balances the male and female energies within oneself.

TELAESTHESIA—visual pictures of an event without the use of the normal physical senses. see clairvoyance

TELAPORTATION—the ability to move objects from one place to another mentally. Movement without physical contact. The ability to move through objects by dematerialization and materialization.

TELEDIAGNOSIS—a term for a distant physical diagnosis of one's health.

TELEKINESIS—also called PK. the ability to move objects without physical aid. An older term used for psykokinesis which is preffered in Europe.

TELEOLOGY—the study of final causes and purposes.

TELEPATHIC CHANNEL—the lines or roads that energy waves of mental messages follow as they pass from one person to another.

TELEPATHIC HYPNOSIS—the ability to hypnotize one through the projection of thought at a distance.

TELEPATHIC LEAKAGE—a form of telepathy between two persons in which the emotionally charged interests in one are mirrored in the other.

TELEPATHY—awareness or responses to another person's thoughts without the use of the physical senses. Mind to mind Mental communications between one or several people without speaking . Communicating mentally regardless of distance.

TELEPLASM—another name for ectoplasm. see ectoplasm.

TELEPORTATION—a spiritual mental form of phenomenon in

which objects move over a distance and\or through other objects. see apport.

TELERGY—the force which is at work in telepathy and other paranormal happenings.

TELETHERAPY—a mental sending or broadcasting of energy from a practitioner to his subject, as in color therapy.

TELETHESIA—perception from a distance through psychic rapport with a place or environment. see clairvoyance.

TELLURIC CURRENT—a electric current in the earth which most psychics believe to be related to poor health, especially if the currents have been put there by humans.

TELLURIUM—metallic tin-white crystals and minerals which aid physical strength when in emergency situations. An aid for the protective mechanism of the self.

TEMPLE—the physical body is believed to be the dwelling place or temple of the soul. The Divine center within the subconscious. A sacred place.

TEMPLE TRAINING—includes every form of training in the development of paranormal abilities.

TEMPLING—bringing God or Deity beliefs together with the inner spirit, the two are "templed" or perfectly joined.

TENSION—an inner striving unrest. A form of physical protection against the unknown. Fear of the spiritual unknown.

TERRITORIAL WARS—the wars similar to the revolt of the slaves, which led to the downfall of Atlantis. see revolt of the slaves.

TETRAGRAM—a magic or spiritual diagram in the

shape of a four pointed star.

TETRAGRAMMATON—the term for the four letter name of God in the Kabala. **(JHVH, IHVH, JHWH, YHVH, YHWH,)** The modern name is Yahweh or Jehovah.

THANATOLOGY—the study of death and death bed wishes. see death bed visions.

THAW MOON—March 20-April 20. Given this name because the warming of the sun made everything begin to move in growth, one of the most spiritual times of the year. The Ancient Greeks called this Moon the "Aneeghee" meaning the opening. see moons.

THENARDITE—white, brown and red double-pyramid structured crystals used to remove the muddiness from the aura. see aura.

THAUMATURGY—the practice of natural laws to bring about phenomenal events, associated with Ancient magic or religio-magic rites. The term is usually associated with witchcraft, sorcery and magic.

THETA—the pre-sleep state where images began to appear in one's mind or psychic eye. The 8th letter in the Greek alphabet.

THEOCENTRIC—having the Divinity as the central interest and ultimate concern.

THEOCRACY—the state of being governed by one that is divinely inspired.

THEOCRAT—one who enjoys living under Divine guidance, either within oneself or governed by officials of Divine guidance.

THEODICY— a defense of the Divinities goodness and omnipotence in view of the existence of evil.

THEOGONY—a study of the origin and the descent of the Divinities or Gods.

THEOLOGIAN—one who studies beliefs of the Deity, both religious and spiritual.

THEOLOGICAL VIRTUES—the three spiritual graces-faith, hope and charity. These virtues draw the soul closer to God.

THEOLOGIZE—to make or give a spiritual significance to an object, person or thing.

THEOLOGY— the study of religious or spiritual beliefs.

THEONOMOUS—one who lives according to spiritual laws. Subject to God's authority.

THEOPHANY—a visible manifestation of a Deity.

THEORY OF INDETERMINACY—the theory that an observed phenomenon is altered by the observation, this makes scientific experiments difficult.

THEOSOPHY—teachings about God and the world, based on mystical insights.

THE OTHER SIDE—a place to which the spirit or soul go after physical death. The spirit world or domain.

THEOSOPHY—a philosophical system which teaches that one can gain knowledge of a spiritual reality through revelation or the practice of the occult. Divine wisdom. Wisdom of religion.

THERAPEUTIC—all avenues which serves to heal both physically or spiritually.

THERMAL AND ELECTROMAGNETIC IMAGES— thought forms of a spiritual entity as opposed to thought forms of a physical body. Much more powerful in the spiritual reality thus creating "spiritual form" instantly.

THIRD EYE—an invisible but sensitive area located between the eyebrows, used to send or receive psychic energy for purposeful reasons. Spiritual visual eye.

THIRD EYE CHAKRA—Inner eye. The spiritual part of the body which one uses for visualization. color-violet, mauve or purple, stone-amethyst, tone-la, gland-pineal gland. See third eye.

THIRD RAY—the Ray of activity and adaptability. see Ray.

THIRD ROOT RACE—the ancient Lemurians belonged to the third Root Race. see race.

THOREAULITE—brown to yellow prismatic crystals which help bring undesired events to an end.

THOR—the Mythological God of Thunder. see thundereggs.

THORN—associated with the Wreath on Christ's head at his death. Also associated with the Egyptain Goddess Neith.

THOUGHT—to form or have in mind. To have as an intention or opinion,. To form an idea. That which is the beginning of an action or physical creation.

THOUGHT FORM—a nonphysical but visible form, created by thought, which exists in the physical or astral planes. An invisible form in its early stages of becoming a physical object. Without physical solidity. see thought.

THOUGHTOGRAPHY—a form of photography where images are mentally and psychically projected onto a film. Laboratory tests have proven this to be successful in 1960 when Ted Serios projected images onto a film by staring into the lens of a Polaroid camera . The ability to photograph mental images.

THOUGHT READING—understanding and seeing what another is thinking. see telepathy, see thought transference.

THOUGHT TRANSFERENCE—the art of transferring one's thoughts to another without the use of physical objects. see Telepathy.
THROAT CHAKRA—a psychic energy point in the throat. Communication chakra. color-blue, stone-blue turquoise, tone-sol.
THREE—the trinity of all life. Man-woman-child. Father-son-holy ghost. Spirit-mind-body. Growth-expression-end result.
THREE DIMENSIONAL—a physical object with width, depth and height. Visible to the physical eye.
THRESHOLD—the connection between the conscious and the subconscious. The Roman god Janus with two faces was said to be the protector of this threshold.
THRONE—an Asian symbol of a place of peace, com pletion or unity.
THRONE MYSTICISM—a form of Jewish mysticism which disputed Christianity..
THROUGHTH—the fourth and first spirit dimensions where the deceased are able to function and observe the third dimension.
THUNDERBOLT—celestial fire. The sceptre or sword of the mythological sky gods, such as Zues. see zeus.
THUNDEREGG—the Ancients believed the thunderegg to be the result of the wrath of the Gods, thrown down to earth because of humans undesired actions. The sons of Thor, the God of thunder. Crystal clusters.
THUNDER MOON—July 23-August 22, named after the strong thunderstorms which are common during these months. The Ancients believed this loud noise to be the voice of their God. see moons.

TIGER EYE—a mineral with a variety of colors, the most common yellow with a dark eye which brings one's spiritual guides closer to one.

TIME—a series of moments one after another. A linear arrangement of movement in the physical reality. Not a material element of the Universe but an illusion. An element of uncertainty in supernormal functions.

TIME BETWEEN INCARNATIONS—many theories, most common theory states that the time between incarnations is dependent on one's karma.

TIME TRAVEL—the art of travelling either backwards or forwards in time when having an out-of-body experience.

TIN—gray to white grains of minerals used to enhance visualization.

TITANS—symbol of the primitive emotions of humankind. Untamed forces. Uncontrolled energies.

TOBACCO—a dried leaf sacred to American Natives. Believed to have supernatural powers with the ability to heal, harm, bring luck and bring misfortune.

TOKEN OBJECT—an object held by a sensitive for the purpose of divination, see psychometry. see divination.

TONAN—a Mexican Aztec belief that this Primary Goddess was transformed into the Lady of Guadalupe after the Spaniards brought the Christian belief to that area. An Ancient Aztec High Goddess.

TONE—a note of the musical scale used to cleanse or tune the chakras. see chakra.

TONING—a group of people chanting a note of the musical scale to cleanse or open a chakra. A chakra cleansing ritual which involves chanting. see tone.

TONGUES—speaking in unknown or unheard of languages. see xenoglossis.

TOPAZ—a wide range of colored crystals used to help one have an insight into another person's personalities. One of the preferred materials used in a dowsing device.

TORCH—symbol of victory , truth and triumph. Emblem of the Goddess Cybele.

TOTEM—an animal with which a person or group of persons identify, and around whose symbol these people develop rituals.

TOUCHES—touches which have no apparent physical means. Being touched by spiritual entities.

TOUCH FOR HEALTH—a form of applied kinesiology which heals the physical body and enhances spiritual growth.

TOURMALINE—a wide range of colors, the crystals aid in balancing the energies of the aura.

TOWER—a symbol of rising above the physical. Believed to represent one's creation or personality.

TRACER EFFECT—a term used to trace or record dreams and how normal daily living corresponds to ones dreams.

TRANCE—a state in which the conscious mind is at rest, thus giving the spiritual realm free reign to carry on it's work through the person who is going to be used as a channel. The departure from the waking and going into the subconscious state.

TRANSCEND—to go through or rise above.

TRANSCENDENTAL-ISM—understanding, concept or knowledge of the realm beyond the awareness of the objective or conscious senses.

TRANSCENDENTAL MEDITATION—a type

of Yoga meditation which is used with a mantra. see yoga.

TRANSFIGURATION—metamorphic power of a medium who assumes bodily characteristics of deceased persons for their representation. see shapeshifting.

TRANSITION—the act of moving from one place to another, as in death and birth.

TRANSITS—the actual motion of the planets through the sky and therefore around the trigger points of the birthchart.

TRANSMIGRATION—the belief that the soul passes from one physical body to another therefore experiencing realities according to its Karma.

TRANSMUTATION—the changing of the vibratory nature, or spiritual manifestation, of a material element (physical body) so that the element is different after the change. see shapeshifting.

TRANSPARENT DIMENSIONAL WARP—an open window type of existence within the psyche of a knowledgeable receiver which allows other realities to be perceived. Used when one is channelling entities or the Deity. see receiver.

TRANSPOSE—to exchange one spirit for another. To place artificially the planets of one person in the houses of another.

TRANSPORTATION—a movement of human bodies by spiritual beings. Suddenly finding oneself in a different location or situation. Many such events documented, especially in the Christian Bible.

TRANSPOSITION OF THE SENSES—the wandering of the senses through the body, such as seeing with the fingers and hearing with the stomach.

TRANSPOSITIONAL CHART—in Astrology, a birthchart with the transposed planets of another person drawn into or outside of the first person's houses.

TRAVELLING CLAIRVOYANCE—a form of clairvoyance in which the sensitive travels mentally to a distant location and describes the events taking place.

TREADMILL EFFECT—many incarnations caused from one's failure to balance the laws of karma. see karma.

TREE OF KNOWLEDGE— Represents good and evil. The five senses. Freedom of choice.

TREE OF LIFE—represents the spiritual point of balance. The secret of immortality.

TREMOLITE—a variety of colored crystals used to understand the energies of the earth in one's own area.

TRIAD—the trinity. The Spiritual person.

TRIAL—an ESP test referring to each single guess at a card, object or symbol.

TRIANGLE—associated with the "Trinity" of the number three. When the apex is upward it represents the male or positive energy, when it is downward, it represents the female or negative energy. Emblem of the Triple Goddess. see trinity.

TRIARCH—a participant in the spiritual work of the Triunes. see triunes.

TRIDENT—a three pronged spear serving in classical mythology as the attribute of a Sea God. Ruthlessness. A tripling of an energy.

TRILOGY OF KARMIC DOCTRINE—the three stages of reaching self realization or the Divinity, 1-cause and effect, 2-retribution and reparation, 3-reincarnation and re-entry.

TRINE—an astrological aspect characterized by a separation of 120 degrees between two planets, symbolizing the process of harmonization.

TRINITY—the Metaphysical belief is the trinity of God, Thought and Man. The Christian is the Father, the Son and the Holy Spirit. The Goddess is maiden, mother and crone.

TRIP—a name given to experiences of altered perceptions, sometimes due to the use of drugs.

TRIPLIODITE—fibrous crystals of many colors used to maintain the trinity of the physical, emotional and spiritual bodies.

TRIPOD—see pyramid.

TRIUNES—a blending of energies by Initiates into patterns which contribute to the evolution of humankind and the well-being of the earth.

TROPICAL ASTROLOGY—the most common use of Astrology which fails to take into account the earth's axis. see sidereal astrology.

TRUMPET—used for the manifestation of direct voice communications. Symbol of fame and glory. Often used at spirit rituals.

TRUMPET MEDIUM—a psychic who produces "spirit voices" through the use of a trumpet at a gathering or seance.

TRUTH—one's own belief. That which is real to one. Guidelines by which one accepts and lives.

TSAVORITE—emerald green crystals and minerals which are used as an aid in clairaudience. see crystals. see clairaudience.

TSIMTSUM—Islamic mystical belief where God is imagined contracting into him\herself in order to make space for the creation.

TSUBOS—points along the meridians where the flow of energy may become blocked. Also known as accupressure and acupuncture points. The body has apx. 360 tsubos points. Their manipulation is thought to release the flow of "Chi."

TUFA—a porous crystal, white in color, used to stimulate artistic qualities.

TUNNEL—many cultures believe that one passes through a spiritual "tunnel" when passing over or dying. Many documented events of such near dying experiences.

TUNING PROCESS—the mental shifting of the mind in preparation for psychic phenomenon. Clearing the mind of all thought.

TURNABOUT—when one see's oneself clearly as one with God.

TURQUOISE—blue minerals which help maintain the health of the physical and spiritual bodies.

TWELVE STEP PROGRAMS AND METAPHYSICS—holistic healers recognized the benefits of the spiritual 12 step programs which began in 1935, which have been successful in helping persons with incurable addictions.

TWENTY SIXTH SENSE—Metaphysical belief that when one is totally aware spiritually, s\he will have developed twenty six senses.

TWIG—a divining rod. A Christian symbol of growth. A Chinese symbol of strength.

TWILIGHT—symbol of change without change within the natural cycle. The half light of morning or evening. The dividing line which joins but also keeps separate dual or opposing forces.

TWINS—many symbolic meanings. Opposites. Equals. Doubling of power. Duality of existence.

TWO—balance. Positive and negative. Man and woman. Day and night. A joining of all kind.

TYPOLOGY—a Chinese system of classifying individuals according to sets of specific criteria for the purpose of healing.

TYPTOLOGY—receiving messages through the tilting of a table.

U

UFO—an unidentified flying object believed to be from another planet or world.

UFO ABDUCTIONS—documented since 1966, Metaphysicians believe UFO's have existed since the beginning of time.Many spiritual masters have been from other planets or galaxies.

ULLMANNITE—metallic gray to white crystals and minerals used to increase the amount of information one can absorb.

UMBANDA—a Brazilian belief combined with the African teachings of Candomble, a religion ruled by women. The white magic of Macumba. see Quimbanda. see Macumba.

UNCONSCIOUS CO-CREATORS—within the belief that one creates one's own reality, the physical part of this reality that was created by one's helper, neighbour or friend. Co-creators are chosen in the pure soul state.

UNDERWORLD—a social sphere below the level of ordinary life. Hades. See Hell.

UNDERWORLD DEMONS—symbolic of a death wish. Negative entities which live in a negative surrounding. Devils.

UNDINE—a feminine entity of the element water. Represents the suit of Cups in the Tarot. Influence of the moon.

UFOCAL—a location where many sightings of UFO's has taken place.

UNICORN—many meanings. A horse-like animal with one horn in the centre of it's forehead. Purity. Chastity. Stealer of maidens.

UNIVERSAL ENERGY—an energy force believed to be the creator of all kind. Having all knowledge. Creator of the life networking.

The Supreme Deity or God.

UNIVERSAL LIFE FORCE—a vital force or energy that transcends time and space, permeates all living and non-living things, and upon which all things are dependent for health, life and vitality. See universal energy.

UNIVERSAL MIND—that which creates and plans all existence's. The consciousness of the Divinity. See divine mind.

UNIVERSE—that which has no beginning or end. Absolute being. The totality of reality. One whole cell.

UNORTHODOX HEALING—healing applied by non-medical means, as in prayer or the laying on of hands.Unexplainable in modern day medical knowledge.

UPIANISHADS—beliefs by Indo-Aryans regarding the ultimate truth and reality of nature. This knowledge was believed to be enough to gain emancipation from the chain of causals and to be absorbed in Brahman. The more advanced Vedas. Hindu scriptures composed from the eighth to second centuries B.C.

URANIZATION—an astrological introspect made by one's Uranus to any point on another's chart, symbolizing the individualization or disruption of the affected point.

URANTIA BOOK—a book of 2097 pages written in 1934 by superhumans who choose to remain anonymous. It presents a picture of the universe which unifies science, philosophy, spirituality and religion in a holistic structure. It also presents the history, origin and destiny of mankind. It teaches the life of Jesus although it contradicts some of the Christian Bible. This book was published in the 1950's.

UVAROVITE—green garnet crystals used to understand the everlasting soul and it's journey through reincarnation.

V

VALKYRIES—the female warrior attendants of the Norse god Odin

VALLEY—symbol of peace, tranquillity, spiritual meeting place. All things good.

VALLHALLAH—the paradise of Nordic mythology. Home of the Nordic Gods.

VAMPIRE—a mythological being known as the "undead" who are believed to be dead but remain, in some unknown sense, to be alive, emerging from the grave by the darkness of night to feed on the blood of the living. A blood sucking ghost.

VANADINITE—yellow to brown to red crystals used to provide clear visions in meditation.

VASE—symbol of the Egyptian Goddess Nu, the mother of creation.

VEHICLE OF VITALITY—a Crookall term to designate the intermediary between the psychic and physical bodies. The Etheric body.

VEDANTA, THE—a term for the philosophy of the Upanishads. The end and goal of the Vedas. The main ideas are-Brahman is reality, the world is illusion and the soul is God. see upanishads.

VEDAS—ancient spiritual writings of India. The main ideas are called Vedanta a Hinduism. See vedanta.

VEGETARIANISM—a diet from which meat has been excluded, believed to enhance spiritual growth and keep open all energy channels.

VEIL—symbolizes virginity, purity, the untouched, the subconscious.

VEINS OF THE DRAGON—the Ancient Chinese believed the earth to be a body and the underground water system to be "the veins of the dragon."

VENUSIFICATION—an astrological introspect made by one's Venus to any point in anothers chart, symbolizing the increased attractiveness or manipulation of the affected point.

VERDITE—a green mineral with colored specks used to gain information from the Ancients of Lemuria.

VESSEL—the human body. Where the soul resides to learn the required lessons of ones incarnation.

VESTAL VIRGIN—those who kept the important symbolical and holy fire burning in the Vestal stand and also served in the ritualistic work. Originally believed to be of Roman origin, later to be of the early Rosicrucian temples. see rosicrucian.

VIBRATION—the speed at which energy moves. Different speeds or vibrations of energy create different objects.

VIBROTURGY—the study of detecting the physical, mental and spiritual condition, or qualities, of one from inanimate objects once in their possession.

VIRGO—the Zodiac sign "the maiden" August 23-September 22.

VISION—a supernatural appearance that conveys a revelation. A picture or experience in the esoteric or psychical reality. A directive in explaining or foretelling the future. A forewarning. Ghostlike.

VISION QUEST—a ritual common to Native Americans for acquiring a guardian angel or supernatural guidance, also undertaken when direction is needed.

VISITANTS—spiritual entities who show themselves to persons for specific reasons, generally helpful. see apparations.

VISUALIZATION—the process of creating or seeing mental images on the esoteric level. To form a mental visual image.

VISUALIZATION THERAPY—the art or study of curing diseases through mental imagery where one sees the disease and works with it until it disappears. Practitioners differ with their techniques.

VITAL FORCE—see psychic force.

VOICE PHENOMENON—a phenomenon in which voice-like sounds are heard on audio cassettes which were not there at the time of recording, usually the voices of deceased persons.

VOICES—spiritual voices clearly heard by persons, generally of a helpful and directive nature. Many such incidents documented in the Christian Bible.

VOLCANIC ASH—used to soothe the emotions and stimulate initiative and independence.

VOLOMETER—an instrument used to measure will as a dynamic power. see will.

VOODOO—a West Indian Witchcraft of African origin. A belief that one is temporarily possessed by a spirit. Also practised in the Caribbean.

VORTEX—the intersection of multiple ley lines which enhances all psychic phenomenon. The center or opening of a spiritual location. Another name for charka. see ley lines, see chakra.

VOWEL SOUNDS—the oldest form of chants to bring about attunement to ones physical and spiritual body. See om.

VULTURE—destruction followed by rebirth. An

vulture

Egyptain symbol for the Great Goddess's destructive/ regenerative powers.

W

WAITING TECHNIQUE—a form of meditation or divination in which one prepares to receive information, then waits for the information to arrive, usually within minutes.

WALK-IN—a highly developed discarnate entity who takes over the body and personality of one who should have passed over or died because of a completed existence. The walk-in heals the body of the one who should have died, and completes his\her chosen existence thus by-passing the birth, child aspects of life. The walk-in has complete memory of the past existence but not the emotions. Walk-ins are allowed into these bodies only if they choose to help humankind.

WALPURGIS NACHT(night)— April 30, also known as May Day, traditionally the date of an important Witch Festival or Sabbat. The Celtic beginning of summer.

WAND—see scepter. One of the suits of the Tarot symbolizing will and power. Continual renewal of life.

WAR—the battle of opposing forces.

WARRIOR—male Ancestors. Male instincts to preserve all things.

WARRIORESS—female ancestor's. The females fighting instincts to preserve all things.

WARLOCK—a sorcerer or wizard in the art of Witchcraft. A male witch.

WARS OF EXPANSION—Atlantean wars which preceded the Territorial Wars in the downfall of Atlantis. see territorial wars.

WATCHERS—Ancients who watch and form a bridge between humankind, spirits and the Divinity.

WATER—universal matter. One of the four elements, water symbolizes subjectivity, emotion, depth and the ability to love. Universal possibilities.

WATER LILIES—symbol of eternal life.

WATER SIGNS—the astrological water signs are Cancer, Scorpio and Pisces.

WATER WITCH—a person who searches or dowses for water. see dowser

WAVELLITE—a mineral with a wide range of colors. Used to better understand the "whole picture."

WAVES—a symbol of movement of creation. The Ancient Chinese believed that Dragons lived in the waves of the Universe.

WEAVING—the continual and ongoing realm of existence.

WEEPING STATUES—the weeping of real tears from an inanimate object or statue, little is known about this phenomenon. see stigmata.

WELL—symbol of depth in understanding the spirit. Purification and healing.

WEST—many cultures believe that when one dies, one must be buried with one's head to the west. Place of the dead.

WEREWOLF—mythological belief of men and women, who at the full moon, turn into a wolf.

WET TRUTH—another term for Earth-mind truth. see earth-mind truth.

WHEAT—symbol of abundance and fertility. Sacred to the Mother Goddess.

WHEEL—spiritual advancement or regression. Symbol of the complete cycle or networking. A sun symbol. Time and movement of karma.

WHEEL OF BIRTH—the need to satisfy karma or

cause and effect. Born for the purpose of a specific experience needed to reach the required end result.

WHIRLWIND—the Ancients believed this to be the wind of the devil. Universal evolution. see devil.

WHITE BROTHERHOOD—an ancient group of highly spiritual people who were very knowledgeable but kept their knowledge secret, it was given to a chosen few. These teachings and knowledge still exist today within true spiritual circles or groups.

WHITE ISLAND OF SHAMBALAH—(Shamballa) a city of the Ancient Gods constructed by the teachers of the race of humankind. see shambalah.

WHITE LIGHT—a universal energy force which can be called upon for healing, protection and all psychic phenomenon. A God energy used for the good of all. Crown chakra color.

WHITE SHEEP— a term given to one who has a strong belief in ESP and the paranormal and also believe they possess this ability. see supersheep.

WHOLISTIC—the whole. Body,mind and soul. A means of Metaphysical beliefs and healing methods.

WICCA—a contemporary Pagan religion with its roots in Shamanism and the earliest expressions of nature and manifestations of the Deity. Among its features are respect of universal energies and the ultimate source of life such as Gods and Goddesses.

WILD ANIMAL MOON—January 19-February 19. Named after the many hungry animals who cannot find food in their natural domains and must come in contact with humans to find food.

WILL—the one and sole principle of abstract eternal. Energy created by desire. The ego.

WILLEMITE—a wide range of colored crystals which promote a welcoming effect to those searching for spiritual answers.

WIND—the active aspects of the Element of Air. Cleansing. Change.

WINDOW—symbol of the eyes, which have been called "windows of the soul".

WINE—symbol of blood and sacrifice.

WINE SKIN—ancient Greek expression "to untie the wineskin" meant to partake of sexual activities.

WINGS—love and victory especially to the Ancient Greeks as seen in their winged Dieties. Spirituality. Rising of spiritual thought.

WINTERLAND—the lower planes of consciousness, the equivalent of the Christian hell. see summerland.

WISDOM—a method of thinking and living in which the holistic values and intuitive process have complete control of one's life and having the best interest of all-kind as one's priority. The understanding and ability to apply knowledge. The personification of the Divine plan.

WISDOM BASED CULTURE—a culture in which the attainment of wisdom is the prime objective of one's existence.

WISE ONES—teachers who have remained on earth to monitor and guide man's progress.

WITCH—many meanings A female who practices magic and folk magic. Black witch is negative, white witch is positive. Female who practices Wicca. See witchcraft.

WITCH OF ENDOR—in the Christian Bible, Book 1, Samuel 28, the witch of Endor was to have called up the ghost of the prophet Samuel at the command of King Saul. The ghost angrily predicted Saul's downfall. apx. 1000 B.C.

WITCHCRAFT—folk magic, spirituality and organized religion. Practical and earthy spells designed to improve the spell-casters life. Wicca. A fast growing movement in the Western World in both negative and positive spiritual realms.

WITCHCRAFT ACT—see Fortune Telling Act.

WITCHDOCTOR—also known as a Shaman. A person, usually a male, thought to possess magical, spiritual and healing powers.

WITCHED—a person or place which has been inspected by a dowser, as in witching one's health. see dowser.

WITCHING—see dowsing.

WITCH'S GARLAND—an Italian belief of the garland being a series of knots with a feather of a black hen inserted at intervals, used to cast spells.

WITNESS EFFECT—an effect resulting in a change of information, received by a medium, because of the energies of the one watching. see theory of indeterminacy.

WITNESS CHAMBER—a chamber built into a dowsing device, into which the dowser places a sample of the target. see target.

WIZARD—one who practices magic or sorcery, usually a male.

WOLF—symbolizes man in the precivilized state. An untamed consciousness.

WOODHOUSEITE—white to pink cubic type crystals used as protection from subliminal suggestions.

WORDS—methods of expression in this physical reality but are "objects" in other realities.

WORK—necessary to attain mental and spiritual growth. Helping others grow spiritually.

WORKSHOP—a place of learning a specific Metaphysical skill, generally one skill at a time.

WORLD TEACHER—the one who holds the concept of the Heirarchy's goals within his\her aura, and is responsible for the training of the angels evolution. see angels.

WORSHIP—to honour or reverence as a divine being. A process by which the soul personality of man becomes consciously aware of its oneness with God.see soul,

WRAITH—an apparition or double of a living person in his own likeness usually seen just before his\her death. see double.

WREATH—symbolizes the circle or cycle of growing things. Continuation of growth.

WRONG—that which does not agree with one's moral standards. A non-spiritual act. A physical error. see right.

X

X—many meanings. The unknown. Place of signature. Location. Spiritual unknown. Spiritual location. Xmas.

X-ENERGY—an energy type that is scientifically known to exist but is not yet isolated from other energies. Psychics believe this to be the energy with which they work.

X-OLOGY—a study of the unknown. A study of one thing and finding something completly different.

X-RAY VISION—the ability to psychically see through objects, walls, etc.

XENOGLOSSY—the ability to speak and understand a foreign or unknown language without learning it. Believed to be the language of a past life.

XENOGRAPHY—the ability to write in a language unknown to the writer.

XENOTIME—a wide range of colored crystals used to assist with creativity and the laws of creativity.

Y

Y-ROD—an instrument used in Dowsing having a "Y" shape, made of wood or steel.

YAHWEH—the name of the personal god from the old testament of the Christian bible. Jehovah.

YANG—a contracting or more organized form of energy. The masculine principle of Taoist philosophy. see yin.

YANTRA—a geometric design type of emblem or instrument of contemplation. A focal point. See mandala.

YEAR—one revolution of the Earth around the sun. Important, especially in Astrology.

YELLOW LIGHT—(energy) Color of the solar-plexis charka. Third color of the rainbow. Color used in healing the mid section of the body. Color used when moving an object towards oneself in the practice of telekinesis.

YETI—see abominable snowman.

YIN—an expanding or becoming more dispersed form of energy. The feminist principle of Taoist philosophy. see yang.

YOD—a Hebrew letter symbolizing the hands of man, power, skill and dexterity.

YOGA—ancient Eastern belief of mind control. A discipline of body positioning with the end result being a feeling of well being.

YOGIS—one who practices yoga. Sanskrit word meaning to bind, join attach or yoke.

YOKE—coupling or uniting. Sacrifice because of its association with the oxen.

YORUBA—a spiritual group of people of Southwestern Nigeria whose magical practices are the bases for many of the new world cults, such as Santeria, Candomble and Trinidad's Shango.

YOUNG SOUL—a soul which has just began incarnating into the physical reality. One who has few physical incarnations or lifetimes.

Z

ZAHORIS--a group of early Spaniards who were highly skilled clairvoyants.

ZANG—an organ concerned with the storage of energy, usually associated with a solid organ like the liver.

ZARATITE—emerald green crystals used to maintain and enhance the energies of the aura.

ZEALOT—one who has fanatical ideas on a subject, not necessarily spiritual.

ZEITGEIST—the spirit of the moment. The consensus of thoughts, feelings and ideas prevailing at any given moment.

ZEN—a Japanese form of Buddhism that dictates a way of living through mind control, by shutting out the material, thus allowing the intuition to grow and build.

ZENER CARDS—cards invented by Dr. Zener in the 1930's, used in ESP testing which have the five symbols: circle, plus sign, rectangle, star or wavy lines as originally used in Duke University.

ZERO—symbolizes the absolute freedom of all limitation. The absence of mass or matter.

ZIGGURAT—a temple tower built by the Sumerians. Found in many parts of the world, consisting of huge stone ladders which persons would climb to meet their Gods. Stone structures built by spiritual beings from other planets as gifts to their Gods.

ZIRCON—a variety of colored crystals used to promote the oneness of oneself and nature.

ZODIAC—an imaginary "belt" in the universe through the middle of which, the sun's path proceeds. It contains twelve signs, each for one month. Astrologers use these signs to foretell one's past, present and future. Most Ancient Nations had the Zodiac holding mysterious messages for those who knew how to interpret them.

ZOMBI—a Haitian word for a corpse reanimated by sorcery and subject to the sorcerer's will.

ZONE THERAPY—reflex healing by massaging zones of the feet and hands which stimulate corresponding horizontal and vertical zones of the body.

ZOROASTER—a 6th century B.C. Persian religious reformer and prophet who influenced the times with his religion of fire worship.

ZOROASTRIANISM—a Persian belief of fire worship founded by Zoroaster (or Zarathustra). Its modern derivation is the Parsee Faith.

REQUESTS

This dictionary is the result of many people sending me words they used or heard.

Please, if you the user, have heard new words that are not in this Metaphysical Dictionary, I would ask that you send them to me. I will enter them at the next printing. This will help us better understand Metaphysics and one another.

Also if you have any comments that you wish to make, or have any questions, please do not hesitate to write. I will certainly answer all letters received.

Write to:
Sunny Tangas
Unit 178
230-1210 Summit Drive
Kamloops B.C. V2C 6M1